Helpful Truth in Past Places

It was J I Packer who likened the Puritans to the Giant Redwoods, now Mark Deckard shows us why. With the skillful hands of a gifted counselor and the inquisitive mind of a pilgrim, Deckard brings us into conversation with these Puritan greats and artfully displays for us their insights into life and relationships. Every Christian counselor, professional or otherwise, ought to pull up a chair and listen in and learn from this conversation.

Stephen J. Nichols, President,
Reformation Bible College, CAO Ligonier Ministries, Sanford, Florida

Before there was a discipline called psychology, many Puritan authors were outstanding biblical psychologists possessed of clear insight to the human frame. Mark Deckard ably distills the essence of 17th century wisdom for 21st century counselors in areas such as God's providence, personal contentment, repentance and depression. I already wonder about a sequel volume, lending this kind of accessibility to more of the existing Puritan treasure trove of practical guidance for Christian living.

Michael A. Rogers, Senior Pastor,
Westminster Presbyterian Church, Lancaster, Pennsylvania

This book is a goldmine for anyone involved in helping hurting people. Mark Deckard takes seven Puritan classics and shows how pastor-preachers wrote them to provide biblical counsel which was profound and balanced, realistic and tender. The principles he extracts are as relevant for the 21st century as when they were first expounded. In these pages is something far better than a 'system' or set of counseling techniques. We are invited instead to gain wisdom – a deeper understanding of people & of how God's grace can change and strengthen them through 'the sufferings of this present time'. That the author stimulates us to read the Puritans with new eyes is a bonus. The final chapter is a marvellously useful summary of how and where to find contemporary counsel from the riches of the past.

Edward Donnelly, Former Principal,
Reformed Theological College, Belfast.

Helpful Truth
in Past Places

The Puritan Practice of
Biblical Counselling

Mark Deckard

MENTOR

ISBN 978-1-84550-545-5

10 9 8 7 6 5 4 3 2

First published in 2010 and reprinted in 2016
in the
Mentor Imprint
by
Christian Focus Publications, Ltd,
Geanies House, Fearn, Ross-shire,
IV20 1TW, Great Britain.

www.christianfocus.com

Cover design by Daniel Van Straaten

Printed by
Bell & Bain, Glasgow

MIX
Paper from
responsible sources
FSC® C007785

CONTENTS

ACKNOWLEDGEMENTS

As with most authors, no book comes about solely because of the actual author. The biblical counseling reflections in this book are the result of twenty-six years of involvement in counseling ministry. Along the way, I have been instructed by many of those I was seeking to help as well as those I worked with. Special thanks goes to Dr John Pugh (now Director of the Graduate Counseling program at Lancaster Bible College) for many years of training and supervisory insight while we served together at Christian Counseling Associates. I also express thanks to many national believers overseas who provided me the opportunity to teach them biblical counseling and in so doing challenged me to think more deeply about what portions of my understanding were Western culture and which were truly biblically derived (a process I am far from completing!).

As to the book itself, I always appreciated the Puritans but did not read them much after my seminary graduation. In recent years, my friendship with Dr Stephen Nichols (Professor at Lancaster Bible College) has challenged me anew with going back to read the Puritans again. And Dr Sinclair Ferguson is probably to be credited with beginning the idea for this book through a lecture he gave on Jeremiah Burroughs that was both theologically deep and pastorally applicable. That prompted me to read Burroughs myself and the journey began.

As for actually sitting down to write, that was a different matter. I've always enjoyed preparing an outline, but not actually writing a narrative. A missionary friend with Christar, Ken Wiest, has been encouraging me to write for years as have my wife and daughter (who writes with much more talent than I do). The actual writing and bringing of production of this book was brought about by Stephen Nichols who not only encouraged but also helped me throughout the process. It is a debt I cannot repay but suspect he does not want me to try to repay it – I only hope my chapter on Jonathan Edwards can pass muster with him. A special word of thanks to Philip Ross of Christian Focus for the painstaking task of reading through the book several times and each time making recommendations for changes that truly enhanced the readability and the accuracy of the text. A final special thank you to Christian Focus for taking a chance on a new, unheard of author and doing the hard work of bringing the book to print.

Finally, I would like to thank my wife, Teresa, of thirty-three years (at the time of writing). She has always been encouraging, loving, and properly confronting to try to help me to be a better servant of our Lord.

Ultimately, all glory belongs to God if this book accomplishes its goal of helping others to be better equipped to help strugglers find God in their difficulty, and thus be able to serve and glorify him through the process of change.

Mark A. Deckard

1

NEW IS NOT NECESSARILY BETTER

The Puritans as Guides for Modern Biblical Counseling

WHY THIS BOOK?

Within the current resurgence of literature about the Puritan writers of the 1600s and 1700s, there has been a useful focus on making their writings more accessible and relevant to the average Christian. The Puritans were masters at understanding the nature of human beings and applying Scripture in practical ways to help people with their struggles and problems. In the truest sense of the word they were psychologists, students of the inner person, before there ever was a field of secular psychology. As such, they have much to offer believers today for their spiritual growth, especially those involved in peer, lay, or professional counseling ministries. This book seeks to explore specifically chosen Puritan books to make direct application of their principles to biblical counseling concerns today. By so doing, it will hopefully encourage believers to revisit these and other Puritan writers in order to be better equipped in their ministry of helping others.

I write from the specific background of a biblical counselor who sees the need for sound biblical understanding to counter some of the shallow psychological understandings that are prevailing in our culture and sadly in Christian circles as well. In addition, I have been involved in training lay counselors, professional counselors, and pastors in the U.S. and overseas in principles of effective biblical counseling. I have found in the reading for this book that the Puritans continually challenge me with more effective ways to help the struggling people I meet. My hope is that you will find yourself similarly challenged and equipped.

Too often today, the past is seen as irrelevant or outmoded and therefore of little use as we attempt to think about and help those struggling with counseling types of problems. The emphasis is always on the new 'finding', the new research, the new medication, the new diagnosis which will suddenly unlock the secrets to people's dark struggles. I am reminded of Dr Jekyll and Mr Hyde in which Robert Louis Stevenson presented this very situation (120 years ago) as Dr Jekyll tries to find the special drug formula that will separate good from evil in people's inner lives and thus free the world from insanity. Of course, his efforts fail in the book and too often today's efforts follow the same storyline. Just as with Dr Jekyll, it is not from a lack of concern or even from a misplaced emphasis on scientific answers. Psychology does at times offer observations and research that helps counselors in terms of understanding the nature of people's struggles and even effective ways to help them in those struggles. But the key area of disagreement always comes back to the foundations – who are people, why do they struggle, what has God provided to help with those problems? Without proper answers to these questions, we build the walls of our house on a shaky foundation. The walls may actually be sturdy in and of themselves but if they have a poor foundation they will ultimately fall to the ground.

It is exactly at this point that we can benefit from looking back to the past, to the great Puritan pastor–theologians. While the Puritan preachers were careful interpreters of Scripture they are also commonly referred to as 'physicians of the soul' because they were equally committed to interpreting their hearers. They knew their theology but they also studied and knew their people. For them psychology, being the knowledge of man, was to be founded in theology as the knowledge of God. And theology was not a study simply for the academic elite but was a subject for all believers. They were sound theologically but did not stop with just propounding theological truth or doctrine, rather they made those doctrines functional in the day to day struggles of the people they taught. And it is important to note that many of these well educated theologians were pastors to day laborers or seafarers, and some, such as John Bunyan, did not have formal academic training. So, the Puritans certainly were trying to bring doctrinal truth to bear in the lives, not of the elite, but of people with day to day problems such as poverty, loss of children, abuse, and alcoholism.

How should we use their approach? Sarles answers, 'By applying the theological truths they employed to the psychological presuppositions of our own day. Their view of how sin dominates the life provides the key to understanding addictive behavior. Their God-centeredness established the framework for a proper approach to self-image.' He quotes Tim Keller of Redeemer Presbyterian Church, New York City:

> By modern standards any person struggling with deep patterns of self-gratification or self-will might be told, 'You aren't responsible' or 'A real Christian wouldn't feel like that' or 'you must have a demon.' By contrast, the Puritan counselor first exhorted the person to mortify the sin through contrition, confession, and repentance. The counselor encouraged the individual that the struggle with sin was a good sign, indicating there was not yet a complete dominance of sin. On this basis there was reason to hope that the pattern of sin would be broken through the truth of the gospel. The English Puritans would be appalled at the emphasis today on self-esteem; they would eschew talk of 'unmet needs,' because in their view the only real need to be met was the need to worship. That is why Puritans practiced sanctification by theology rather than by psychology.[1]

---

1 Ken L. Sarles, 'The English Puritans: a Historical Paradigm of Biblical Counseling' in *Introduction to Biblical Counseling*, ed. John F. MacArthur, Jr. and Wayne Mack (Dallas: Word, 1984), 28.

The Puritans understood clearly that underlying heart motives and desires drive our behavior and must be addressed for true growth through problems to occur. But they were also sensitive to the varying causes for personal problems – physical, spiritual, temperamental and demonic – so they provide us with a truly holistic way of trying to look at people in difficulties rather than an imbalance that focuses only on one of these areas (true in secular psychology circles, biblical counseling circles and also in spiritual warfare thinking). It is a balanced approach, but one with a firm foundation in the teaching of Scripture.

WHO WERE THESE PURITANS?

Originally, Puritan was a reference to those who wanted to purify the worship and teaching of the Church of England in the late 1500s and 1600s. But it soon grew to be a term that referred to a movement and a somewhat unified body of belief. It was not a strictly unified body of doctrine, however, for among the Puritan ranks were Anglicans (William Perkins, Richard Sibbes), Separatists (William Bradford), Independents (Thomas Goodwin, John Cotton, John Owen), Presbyterians (Thomas Watson) and Baptists (John Bunyan). Puritan came to describe more a group of people firmly committed to the authority of Scripture in all areas of life, and living lives dedicated to the glory of God. And some are included (Thomas Boston and Jonathan Edwards) who lived after the time of the formal Puritan dissent had concluded in 1689 with the Act of Toleration in England.

Historically, there was an ebb and flow to the Puritan movement as they went through periods of being the dominant religious voice in England to periods of persecution. After the reign of the Catholic Queen Mary in which Protestants were persecuted, many returned to England with the rule of Queen Elizabeth (1533–1603). But many felt that Elizabeth's Acts of Uniformity (1559) only 'half-reformed' the church and so voices such as Thomas Cartwright began to be heard seeking for deeper, genuine reform. In 1593 the Act Against Puritans was issued which removed many of these 'Puritans' from their pulpits. They continued teaching wherever they could. In 1603, James I, a Calvinist, became King but the situation did not improve as James yielded to the idea that his political power as King was linked to the established church structure (the King being seen as the Supreme Head of the Church of England). More ministers were suspended and many left for the Netherlands. James I did ease the pressure as his reign continued.

But he was followed by Charles I, a Catholic King, whose advisor William Laud began to exercise religious control beginning in 1628. With the dissolving of Parliament in 1629 Bishop Laud was free to exercise his persecution of Puritans to the fullest. This produced another exodus of Puritan leadership to the Netherlands and to New England (led by John Winthrop to Massachusetts). Many others followed to New England (John Cotton, Thomas Hooker, Thomas Sheppard) starting the historical trend that culminated in the ministry of Jonathan Edwards in the 1700s.

Finally, Charles' persecution brought about a Civil War in which the Puritan, Oliver Cromwell, led the forces of the Parliament (which Charles I had dissolved) to victory. It was during the Civil War (1642–48) that the re-established Parliament brought together over one hundred Puritan leaders at Westminster Abbey where they drafted the still utilized *Westminster Confession of Faith*. Cromwell ruled as Lord Protector until 1658 and allowed religious freedom so that all religious groups flourished and grew, including the Puritans with whom he identified personally. However, the monarchy was restored in 1660 by Charles II who initially promised liberty of religious conscience, but instead pushed for religious conformity. It was during this time of persecution that John Bunyan found himself imprisoned. The 1662 Act of Uniformity demanded that Puritan ministers renounce their denominational ordinations and be re-ordained by the bishops. Those who refused (thousands of them) were removed from their churches. This was followed by the Conventicle Act in 1664 which banned nonconformists from preaching in fields or homes, and then in 1665 by the Five Mile Act which prohibited the ejected ministers from coming within five miles of their former churches or any city or town. It was a time when much of the Puritan preaching was silenced, but as authors they continued to speak through the written word.

The Puritans were unified in their basic commitment to Scripture and glorifying God, and in their experience of persecution and often exile. Gleason and Kapic note seven basic core beliefs they all shared:

1. Understanding Puritanism as a movement of spirituality.
2. Laying stress on experiencing communion with God.
3. United in their dependence upon the Bible as their supreme source of spiritual sustenance and guide for reformation of life.
4. Were predominantly Augustinian in their emphasis upon human sinfulness and divine grace.
5. Placed great emphasis upon the work of the Holy Spirit in the believer's life.
6. Were deeply troubled with sacramental forms of Catholicism spiritually fostered within the Anglican Church.
7. Can be understood as a revival moment.[2]

WHAT ABOUT TODAY?

The Puritans combined being students of the Word of God, not just in an academic way (although many were professors at colleges and universities), but with also being experiential. They never allowed experiential to supersede Scripture as the ultimate authority but neither did they see sound doctrine as divorced from an experiential Christian life. They learned who their people were and taught them Scripture in ways that would help them go through their day to day struggles, finding contentment and strength for the journey of the Christian life. And despite our modern prejudices, their problems were not all that different than our own. Application is certainly needed for the twenty-first century but the basic struggles of fear, depression, spiritual warfare, and explaining a seemingly chaotic and random world were all problems in their day as well as ours. And because of the persecutions they individually suffered, they speak

2 Randall Gleason and Kelly Kapic, 'Who were the Puritans?' in *The Devoted Life – An Invitation to the Puritan Classics*, (Downer's Grove: InterVarsity Press. 2004), 24–30.

with a genuineness of having experienced these problems in their own lives and ministries. They truly do offer us helpful truth in past places and we ignore their contributions at our own personal loss, but also to the detriment of those we seek to help as they fight through their overwhelming problems in today's world.

The Puritans are admittedly rather difficult for modern readers to digest. This is partly due to the cultural and historical differences but also to their general style of writing which would probably be considered flowery and verbose in modern writing circles. This is coupled with a deep theological content that frankly makes them hard to understand, much as Peter writes of the Apostle Paul in 2 Peter 3:15–16, 'just as our dear brother Paul also wrote you with the wisdom that God gave him. He writes the same way in all his letters, speaking in them of these matters. His letters contain some things that are hard to understand...' Peter struggled to understand Paul at times but he kept on reading him. In a similar way, the Puritan writers can be difficult to understand in the depth of their concepts but they are worth the struggle. It is my hope that I can help bring seven of these key authors and their books to a point where we can understand their basic applications to counseling problems today. In so doing, their teaching from the past will live on as useful not only in the lives of their original hearers or readers, but also in the lives of believers today.

I have sought to diligently read the Puritans with the specific question of biblical counseling in mind. While they are worth reading purely at a theological level, it would be a disservice to them to leave them solely at that level. As previously noted, they were concerned to be physicians of the soul, bringing biblical truth and doctrine to the lives of fellow strugglers so as to assist them in the journey, as well as keep them progressing in the work that God wanted to do in their lives. Where possible I have changed some of the more archaic words in quotations from the authors but have otherwise allowed their words to stand on their own with the interpretations and applications being mine.

I have found this personal journey convicting. As I read and wrote, I was trying to think of how I might equip others to use these wonderful resources to be more effective in people's lives today and I hope that goal is achieved. But I also repeatedly experienced personal conviction and encouragement as I thought upon what these men of God were saying some 350 years ago! I hope your journey is a similar one and that if you are not already a fan of the Puritans you may take a stab at reading one or two of them directly without the intervention of myself or another interpreter.

2

WHY IS THIS HAPPENING TO ME?

God's Providence in our Struggles[1]

'I will cry out to God Most High,
to God, who fulfills his purpose for me.'
(Ps. 57:2)

John Flavel was born in 1627 as the son of a Puritan pastor. After studying at Oxford he began his ministry as an assistant pastor and then after six years moved to Townstall church in the seaport of Dartmouth to be their pastor, at a loss of pay! In 1662 he was driven out of his ministry by the Act of Uniformity, and prohibited from living in the area by the Five Mile Act of 1665. Although some ministers took the oath required by the Act, Flavel refused, and instead moved to a location outside the five mile limit. Many of his congregation resorted to coming to see him there to be ministered to and a 5 mile

---

1 This chapter is based on John Flavel, *The Mystery of Providence*. Unless otherwise indicated, all quotations come from the 2002 reprint published by the Banner of Truth Trust.

journey was much more of an adventure in their day than in ours. At the same time, his parents were arrested in London on a charge of sedition and sent to the infamous Newgate Prison. Although they eventually were bailed out, it was too late as they had contracted the plague while in Newgate and died from the disease. Flavel was able to return to his church in Dartmouth in 1672 but was again driven out in 1682, moving to London this time. He finally returned to his congregation in 1687 and ministered there until his death in 1691.

Flavel was a prolific writer, with his complete works comprising six volumes. *The Mystery of Providence* was first published in 1678. Flavel was personally acquainted with the struggles inherent in trying to believe that God is providentially guiding events. When *The Mystery of Providence* was first published he had lost his first wife and unborn child in labor and although he had remarried, his second wife would also precede him in death. Two more marriages would follow with only his fourth wife actually outliving him. This was coupled with his experiences of ministry exile and the tragic loss of his parents.

His writings and ministry were marked by a desire to present theological truths by applying them to the day to day struggles of his people. Many stories exist of unique occurrences related to his ministry efforts. One of these will illustrate not only how God used Flavel's preaching and teaching but also the Providential working of God which he wrote about.

> There are some remarkable examples of the effects of Flavel's ministry. Luke Short was a farmer in New England who attained his hundredth year in exceptional vigor though without having sought peace with God. One day as he sat in his field reflecting upon his long life, he recalled a sermon he had heard in Dartmouth as a boy before he sailed to America. The horror of dying under the curse of God was impressed upon him as he meditated on the words he had heard so long ago and he was converted to Christ – eighty-five years after hearing John Flavel preach.[2]

Is Flavel, and this book in particular, still relevant to the modern day church? At first glance it appears to be a subject that we mention

---

2 Boland, *Publishers' Introduction* to The Mystery of Providence (Carlisle, PA: Banner of Truth Trust, 1963), 11.

but rarely focus upon. We tend to focus today on questions such as, How can I feel happy, or How can I know what job God wants me to have? If we feel at peace in these questions, we rarely look deeper into the mysteries of God. In contrast, Flavel calls us to both seek out the works of God's providence and then also meditate upon them! Why the difference? Writing forty years ago, Michael Boland noted that today we tend to approach providence in a superficial way, simply quoting Romans 8:28, 'God works all things together for good' but only in the good times, not in the truly difficult events of life. Secondly, he noted we tend to have a distaste for meditation in general, it is not a common practice for believers today.[3]

Responding from the perspective of the counseling ministry, Boland is correct on both counts. Actually, it could be stated further as being not so much an ignoring of these two important truths but an actual ignorance of them due to lack of teaching on the subjects. Thus Flavel's writing is urgently needed by Christians today to return us to a proper understanding and use of God's providence in our lives, not only that we may grow daily but also that we might truly discover how God can work through our trials and problems to bring peace and comfort into our lives. To recognize that the true goal of counseling is not necessarily to remove the suffering but rather to grow through the suffering, requires an understanding of God's providence. Of course, the first step for many in the counseling setting, both counselors and counselees, is to accept that the immediate relief of suffering is not always possible and is not necessarily the initial goal of counseling. Flavel points us to this understanding in his writing.

The first question that will come to the mind of the modern struggler is, what is providence anyway? The word pops up from time to time in titles and even in a television show here and there (it has appeared as the name of a small, distant town in television Westerns or Science Fiction movies on occasion) but most have little idea of what it truly means. Interestingly, Flavel does not actually attempt a definition although he will distinguish providence from sovereignty (providence being divine sovereignty as it is acted out in

---

3 Ibid., 12–13.

our lives) later in the work. For him and his time, the presence and concept of providence seems to have been a given, so that his attempt is to defend providence from the attacks of critics who deny it, and then to help believers understand how to allow providence to have its 'perfect work in their lives.'

A rather lengthy but encompassing definition that fits well with Flavel's use would be:

> Providence is normally defined in Christian theology as the unceasing activity of the Creator whereby, in overflowing bounty and goodwill (Psalm 145:9, cf. Matthew 5:45–8), He upholds his creatures in ordered existence (Acts 17:28; Colossians 1:17; Hebrews 1:3), guides and governs all events, circumstances and free acts of angels and men (Psalm 107, Job 1:12, 2:6; Genesis 45:5–8), and directs everything to its appointed goal, for his own glory (cf. Ephesians 1:9–12).[4]

For the counselor and the struggler, providence turns out to be a singularly important doctrine, albeit a difficult one to believe in during the time of difficulty. The struggler will wrestle with the notion that God can not be guiding events otherwise they would not be struggling, and at times the counselor may also feel that if God was truly guiding events then there should be progress in the counseling. After all, if God is really good then he would bring happiness in our lives, and if he is all-powerful then isn't he capable of doing so? At least that is how the questions form in our minds as we come face to face with struggle, tragedy, and injustice. Learning to work with the abuser who continues to abuse, the person using drugs who worsens, or the marriage that plummets toward divorce, raises questions of whether God is active, for the counselor as well as the counselee. Practically speaking, it often raises the even more direct question of whether 'this Bible stuff' really works? Trying to point the person experiencing abuse beyond the abuse to recognize that God is still somehow at work is extremely difficult and if done poorly could place an additional burden upon the already struggling

---

4 'Providence' in the *Illustrated Bible Dictionary*, vol. 3 (Wheaton: Tyndale House Publishers, 1980), 1292.

individual. But to ignore the doctrine is to lose a great source of comfort as well as guidance in the midst of trials.

Flavel divided his work into three major sections, the first describing evidences of the working of providence. In his day, while providence was most likely a culturally accepted understanding on the one hand, there were nonetheless many critics arising. Those critics entail a much larger number today, plus the majority of believing Christians either are unaware of the concept of God's providence or tend to describe it in terms closer to fatalism (that all events will proceed in their predetermined way regardless of what I might do). So we will skim through his various evidences to see how they can help point struggling believers towards the actions that demonstrate God at work in their life in the past and in their present struggles. Secondly, Flavel describes how to meditate upon God's providences. Meditation is a rarely practiced skill today, so much of his description may seem foreign to modern believers' ears, but he distinctly shows the importance of focusing upon and meditating upon God's providential acts in order to find strength in the present day struggles we face. Finally, his third section seeks to provide application of the Doctrine of Providence, which in his case ends up being an effort to demonstrate the benefits of focusing upon providence as well as the dangers of not doing so.

INTRODUCTION TO PROVIDENCE

While we often feel God is distant and may even raise the question of whether he exists at all during times of struggle, Flavel immediately points us to the necessity of realizing how desperately needed is the presence of God in this crazy world.

> The greatness of God is a glorious and unsearchable mystery (Ps. 47:2). It is the great support and solace of the saints in all the distresses that befall them here, that there is a wise Spirit sitting in all the wheels of motion, and governing the most eccentric creatures and their most pernicious designs to blessed and happy issues.

At the outset, Flavel challenges his readers to think for a moment of a world in which there is no God at work, causing all things to ultimately work together for the good. In the midst of tragedy or deep struggles with anxiety or depression it may seem that there is no God present or at least not working things together for good (a more deistic, a detached God if you will), but what if there truly was no God or he was disinterested in the events of this world? Then we truly would have no hope as we would be tossed by the capriciousness of people and events, and if we lack the power of strength, wealth, or resources then we would be hopeless other than to grit our teeth and just keep struggling onwards to an uncertain end.

Actually the advice to just grit your teeth has been offered, but it raises the obvious question – keep struggling on for what purpose – if there is no purpose, then why bother? Christians rightly see suicide as a choice we do not have the right to make because God is the one who presides over life and death decisions. But the suicidal person feels that God is not present (at least not in their circumstances) and runs out of strength to just keep gritting their teeth. If there is no God at work and thus no ultimate purpose in life, then suddenly suicide actually takes on the appearance of a reasonable option. Understanding providence begins not just by understanding God is over all things and at work in this world, but by understanding that providence is integrally connected to the idea of God's purpose and hence that our lives are purposeful even when they do not feel like it. And with an ultimate sense of purpose, only then does suicide become a thoroughly wrong moral choice.

This question actually was the turning point in my own conversion to Christ. I was not in a time of struggling, rather I was about to head off to a prestigious college and then into a most likely profitable career. But as I considered Christians I had met and one in particular (she is now my wife of over thirty-three years) they seemed to have a purpose and a joy that I lacked. I still remember asking the question, after twenty-five or thirty years of a successful career, I will die and then what, what would it all be for? Without purpose, life is empty and meaningless, and apart from God's presence, all purposes we seek are short-lived and quickly fade away. Similarly, in terms of counseling I have often commented that I am not sure how non-Christian counselors are able to keep going with people who seem to have intractable problems, showing little improvement, or with those who are facing incredible tragedies in their lives. Without a sense that there is a God who knows and makes sense of this world, and has the control that we lack, how can anyone keep going?

This is exactly Flavel's point. To realize there is a God who is intimately involved in the activities of the creation is to bring comfort, knowing we are not alone and are not called upon to do the impossible. But Flavel also immediately introduces us to the idea of mystery. Providence is a mystery. We can see it operating, we can speak of it theologically, but in the end it is part of the mystery of God that results from the divide between Creator and creature. We understand in part, but not fully. I am reminded of the words of Jacob the baker in the writing of Noah ben Shea:

> 'There was a great teacher,' said Jacob, 'who told us that life was like a tapestry. I wondered about this for a long time,' said Jacob. 'And then, watching you over the last days, I discovered that one works on a tapestry from the back. That you work on it without seeing the larger pattern. That all you see are the colored stitches running at odds and at angles to each other. That, indeed, is like life: One day is woven into the next. But we cannot see the implication of every stitch in time. And so we work blind. Courage is the required pattern in life. Courage and faith.'[5]

We may be blind at times but God sees both sides of the tapestry and even sees the finished product (Rom. 8:29–30). Usually counselees desire full explanations of their problems, their situations, and how certain efforts will work out in the future. While I would love to provide those explanations as much as they would like to have them, the initial key is to recognize that while we can explain and understand in part, there is always a degree of mystery about the working of God in our lives. Accepting this by faith will allow us to grow with what God has provided rather than focusing on what we do not understand, and as Flavel will go on to demonstrate, rational attempts of the creature will always fall short of understanding the true nature and working of God and run the risk of leaving the

---

5   Noah ben Shea, *Jacob's Ladder* (New York: Ballantine Books, 1997), 120.

individual in an atheistic state. Not atheistic in the sense of denying the presence of God, but atheistic in the sense of believing that we are the center of the universe and the ones who can explain and define all that is true. Instead, our search for truth must always be rooted in discovering truth as God knows and reveals it to us. But as the only God, it would be expected that we, as created beings, will never know all that he knows. Thus, alongside the search for truth and solutions in the counseling setting, appears the idea of mystery, that we can never fully understand the 'why' questions of what is happening and what God is doing. Fortunately, an understanding of providence tells us that we do not have to understand them completely in order to find comfort and strength to continue on.

While those who are struggling often feel that no one can understand their struggle (I have heard that spoken verbally and nonverbally hundreds of times), Flavel demonstrates this is not true. Throughout his book he provides illustrations from the lives of his time and culture, but even more so he constantly brings in Scriptural descriptions of genuine struggles. Commenting on the verse that forms the foundation for his discussion, Psalm 57, he notes: 'Three things are remarkable in the former part of the Psalm, his extreme danger; his earnest address to God in that extremity; and the arguments he pleads with God in that address.' David was hiding in a cave in the wilderness of Engedi to avoid the vengeance of King Saul (1 Sam. 24:1–2). But now he finds himself in the cave with Saul's army camped nearby and no other outlet from the cave but that which faced the enemy. Then King Saul enters the mouth of the cave so that discovery and a hopeless fight seem imminent. Facing potential destruction, David cries out to God in a situation of great distress.

> First, he pleads his reliance upon God as an argument to move mercy. 'Have mercy on me, O God, have mercy on me, for in you my soul takes refuge' (v. 1). He pleads former experiences of his help in past distresses as an argument encouraging hope under the present difficulty: 'I will cry out to God Most High, to God, who fulfills his purpose for me' (v. 2)...Upon this he acts his faith in extremity of danger. Saul is high, but God is the most high, and without his

permission he is assured Saul cannot touch him. He had none to
help, and if he had, he knew God must first help the helpers or they
cannot help him.

For David, God's past workings on his behalf become the foundation
for his faith that God would continue to be with him in the current
trial that he faced.

David's distress, seeking of God, and deliverance by God
(eventually replacing Saul as king) are recorded in Scripture that
we might be encouraged by them today (1 Cor. 10:6). In essence,
these historical events of Scripture lift the 'veil' on providence to
show us how God has worked in the past with the promise that he
will continue to act according to his nature in the present. At the
time of David's deliverance he had already been promised the future
kingship by God, yet it did not occur at the time of this deliverance
but much later. God's deliverance is one of the proofs that the
promised kingship will one day occur, but David is left in mystery as
to when and how that will take place. 'Grace makes the promise, and
providence the payment.' God's promises are often mysterious to us,
we try to rest in them and claim them in our lives but feel they are not
appearing. Sometimes we even try to make them occur. This was the
reaction of Abraham when faced with God's seemingly unfulfilled
promise of a son (Gen. 15). He and Sarah chose to follow a common
custom of the day to have a child through Sarah's slave (Gen. 16),
who would then be considered to be Sarah's offspring. But this was
not the manner in which God intended to bring about his promise.
The strife that has occurred between the descendants of Isaac and
Ishmael unfortunately continues to this day. Rather God, in his own
providential timing brought the birth of Isaac about in a supernatural
way (Gen. 21). His providence made the payment upon the previously
declared Promise. It is not our role to devise our ways of bringing
about what we perceive God's will to be in our lives, but rather to
trust in him and seek his guidance for today's steps towards the
future promises he has provided.

But someone might claim that David and Abraham were important
people in the outworking of God's plan, does God really care about

the 'unimportant people' of life, and the trivial events of our lives? Flavel answers with a resounding Yes!

> This expression imports the universal interest and influence of Providence in and upon all the concerns and interests of the saints. It not only has its hand in this or that, but in all that concerns them. It has its eyes upon everything that relates to them throughout their lives. From first to last. Not only the great and more important, but the most minute and ordinary affairs of our lives are transacted and engaged by it. It touches all things that touch us, whether more nearly or remotely.

No struggling person is ever alone, they may feel alone, people may even desert them, but God is always at work. It may be hard to grasp this from how they feel, it requires the act of faith to grab hold of the fact that God is with them in their circumstances and is working in their circumstances, they are not a rudderless, propulsion-less boat being tossed by the waves and currents. It certainly may feel and look that way to them, and to the counselor as well, but faith looks back at the past workings of God to say, it is not so – he is at work now and I will struggle to grasp that truth by faith. And no incident or event is so trivial that it does not fall under the concern of God's providence. In counseling it is often correcting the little things that eventually brings resolution. Wise counseling does not ignore the small or seemingly unimportant events of life, but seeks to challenge people to faithfully seek to serve God in the large and the small occurrences of their lives.

In our world today, history is often cast aside, with the emphasis being on the present and what will happen tomorrow. Scripture, however, has always been concerned with the past, not to try to change it or seek to live in it, but to remember from the past important lessons for today. Memorials figure prominently in Scripture as a means to cause us to stop and reflect upon what God has done and then ask how that God of the past will continue to work his promises today. Remembering how God has worked in the past is essential to being able to grasp how he is working now in the present, in our time of 'darkness.'

Flavel describes two vantage points from which we can see this work of God in our lives. 'One is entire and full, in its whole complex and perfect system. This blessed sight is reserved for the perfect state. The other sight is particular and imperfect which we have on the way to glory, during which we only view it in its single acts, or at most, in some branches and more observable series of actions.' He had helped too many hurting people not to realize that we are unable to see fully or clearly in the present circumstances so as to understand how God's providence is working events and actions around us. Glimpses into Scripture point us to that work, as in the birth, life, death and resurrection of Christ in which so many actions all come together for our salvation. Scripture records these to encourage us in our understanding of how God does work, but also to stir up our faith that just as the twelve disciples struggled at the time to understand what was happening (it looks obvious to us as we read the Gospels from the perspective of two thousand years past their time), so too we may struggle to understand how God is working today in our problems and hurts. But regardless of our level of understanding, we must continue to believe in that providential working of God.

In a point he develops more deeply, Flavel also reminds us that we must seek in the Scriptures, in history, and in our own personal history to reflect back upon what God has done, 'from the text then you have this doctrine: It is the duty of the saints, especially in times of difficulties, to reflect upon the performances of providence for them in all the states and through all the stages of their lives.' He notes the value of 'memorials' that point us back to the works of God as illustrated in Exodus 17:14–15; Esther 9:28, Genesis 28:18–19, and Genesis 16:13–14, for example, and for believers today in the celebration of the Lord's Supper, which serves to point us back to the work of God in Christ on the cross so as to remind us that he who did such a great work for us in the past will continue it today (1 Cor. 11:26). Counselors have often discovered the benefit of urging those they help to keep journals or diaries during protracted times of struggle. These are to help bring a sense of balance as to what God has done. I have encouraged those struggling with depression to keep a simple daily log of whether they felt good, felt neutral, or felt truly depressed, and why. When they do so, many discover that their times of depression are not as numerous as they at first believed. Does this lift the depression? No, but it does bring a balance to help them learn to struggle not only with the down times but also to remember the times that God brought more 'sunshine' into their lives. Like all of us, as the struggle lengthens in time, they tend to lose sight of the good things of the past (quite common in troubled marriages). Learning to reflect upon how providence has worked in the past in our lives and the lives of other believers is Flavel's suggested antidote to this dilemma.

'EVIDENCES OF PROVIDENCE'

Flavel answers directly to those critics who discount providence, claiming perhaps that all happens by chance (the philosophical direction flowing out of Darwinian evolution today) or everything happens by what we choose to do or say (secular humanistic approaches). He poses and answers a series of questions to illustrate the presence of providence in life. For the counselee becoming lost in their struggles, feeling there is no way out, these questions can point them beyond their immediate problem to instead reflect on what God has done so that they may have a greater sense of what he can and will do now and into the future. Flavel is asking each of us if we realize how blessed we are by God. Most of the time we live in ignorance of this question and too often at other times answer that we are not blessed based on our perception of the struggle.

> How comes it to pass that so many signal mercies and deliverances have befallen the people of God, above the power and against the course of natural causes, to make way for which there has been an obvious suspension and stop put to the course of nature?

Too many unexplainable events throughout history have in some way benefited the people of God. While efforts are often made to explain them, such as scientific efforts to explain the miracles of God through Moses in Egypt and the events of the Exodus, these efforts fall terribly short. Granted some make sense and could be even true (but they typically ignore the fact that God may initiate miracles by using the natural resources of his creation, the miracle lies in the timing and how those natural resources come together) but too often they result in rather ridiculous conclusions. There are just too many unexplainable events and reactions by believers to discount the presence of God being at work.

> IT is undeniably evident that there are marvelous co-incidences of Providence, confederating and agreeing, as it were, to meet and unite themselves to bring about the good of God's chosen. He that carefully reads the history of Joseph's advancement to be the lord of Egypt may number in that story twelve remarkable acts or steps of Providence by which he ascended to that honor and authority. If but one of them had failed, in all likelihood the event had done so too, but every one occurred in its order, exactly keeping its own time and place. So in the Church's deliverance from the plot of Haman, we find not less than seven acts of Providence concurring strangely to produce it.

The story of Joseph in Genesis 36-50 and the book of Esther are perhaps the two best extended narratives in Scripture of God's providential working in the lives of specific people. Asking a struggling person to read them, trying to place themselves in the position of Joseph, or Esther and Mordecai is a powerful exercise in helping them to understand how God can be at work now in their life, even if they can not see the specifics of that activity. All three of these individuals pushed ahead to serve God even when all seemed to be lost. For Joseph, the best illustration of his adult life would be of a constant roller-coaster ride as life seemed doomed and tragic, and then hope arises, only to be crushed again. He experienced this up and down ride numerous times but kept on faithfully, and looking back on his life he was able to explain to his brothers that 'you intended to harm me, but God intended it for good to accomplish what is now being done, the saving of many lives' (Gen. 50:20). The strugglers I seek to help would like me to be able to explain how everything will turn out now, for them the narrative of Joseph is a place to find a kindred spirit who truly experienced and knows the feelings they are experiencing and points them to the faith of 'perseverance' (Heb. 12:1–3) through the times when we cannot see clearly and wonder if God has left us.

> I F the concerns of God's people are not governed by a special Providence, how is it that the most apt and powerful means employed to destroy them are rendered ineffectual, while weak, contemptible means employed for their defense and comfort are crowned with success?

Atheists and false religions have sought to eliminate Christianity for centuries but always fail in the end. They may experience temporary 'victories' but over the long term of history Christianity continues to flourish and spread and bring about truly amazing change and hope in the lives of millions. Why would this be, if God was not at work? And if this is so, why would God stop now and abandon one of his children to destruction? It may feel like destruction, as if our enemies or the forces of disease are going to win, but that would mean God is no longer working as he did before. But he is working, for he is the unchanging One (the only unchangeable point in our crazy universe).

> I F all things are governed by the course of nature and force of natural causes, how then comes it to pass that, like a bowl when it strikes another, men are turned out of the way of evil, along which they were driving at full speed? Good men have been going along the way to their own ruin, and did not know it, but Providence has met them in the way and preserved them by strange diversions, the meaning of which they did not understand till the event revealed it.

How is it that so often apparently random events bring people to faith in God (Acts 8:26–9, Naaman in 2 Kings 5:1–4)? For the person struggling to live through each day because of their depression, grief, anxiety, or fear we need to encourage them to consider that we truly do not know the next hour let alone tomorrow. Anxiety in particular leads to the practice of catastrophizing, looking to the worst possible next sequence of events, but God demonstrates over and over in history and Scripture that he can and does intervene with actions totally unexpected by the people experiencing them. The Apostle Paul certainly did not expect to experience a direct encounter with God on the road to Damascus. His goal was to find and bring more Christians to execution for believing in Christ, but instead he suddenly found himself brought down to humbly admit the truth that Christ was the promised Savior of mankind! As he woke that morning and prepared for the day, there is no way he could have predicted that it would turn out the way it did.

> IF these things are contingent [determined and based on other factors preceding them], how is that they fall out so remarkably in the nick of time, which makes them so greatly observable to all that consider them? And, were these things accidental and contingent, how can it be that they should fall out so immediately upon and constantly to the prayers of the saints? So that in many Providences they are able to discern a very clear answer to their prayers, and are sure they have the petitions they asked (1 John 5:15)?

The question should not be why do my prayers seem to go unanswered, but why do any prayers work to have an effect on events? Many events that occur could perhaps be explained as 'chance' and it is true that many prayers seemingly go unanswered. But the more important point is that many prayers are clearly and directly answered in ways observable to many (sometimes even to unbelievers). If there is no providential work present, why would these events occur at the times they do exactly when godly people are praying for them to occur? Prayer is effective even when we can not discern those immediate events. Too often in counseling situations we offer prayer in an obligatory sense as something that Christian counselors should do. Flavel challenges us to remember that prayer is part of the outworking of providence in the lives of those we seek to help, and so prayer is not an add-on but an essential part of directing them back to the God who will ultimately make the difference in their struggle, and already knows the progression of events in their life.

In all these questions, Flavel implicitly points to the necessity of having an historical perspective, and a distinctly memorial perspective as well. He challenges us to look at biblical history as recorded in Scripture but also at the history of the church, and even our own spiritual history. While much may still remain unexplained – there is still mystery this side of heaven – these reflections will force any honest observer to admit that God has been, is, and will continue to be at work ordering events to produce the results that are ultimately the best for his children. Can the existence of God and his providential working be proved as an absolute certainty? No they cannot, but the evidence for both is so overwhelming to a nonbiased observer, that there can be no true question of his existence and his ongoing work in the world. This has often been the experience of my own life. When I find myself lapsing into complaining or thinking that the Christian life is not yielding beneficial results for me, God urges me to reflect back upon what I have seen him do in my own life and in the lives of others. The obvious conclusion is always the same – he is at work, even if I do not know how in my present time of complaint.

PROVIDENCE AT WORK

Flavel illustrates providence with specific events from the lives of his people.

> Consider how well Providence has performed the first work that ever it did for us: in our formation and protection in the womb (Ps. 139:15).

> In nothing does Providence shine forth more gloriously in this world than in ordering the occasions, instruments and means of conversion of the people of God. However skillfully its hand had molded your bodies, however tenderly it had preserved them and however bountifully it had provided for them, if it had not also ordered some means or other for your conversion, all the former favors and benefits it had done for you had meant little.

Providence is at work in our actual creation, the incredible beings that we are when honestly considered. Yet, to be created as a marvelous creation would be pointless if sin remained in our lives to bring destruction in this life and eternal death for eternity. Thus God works events to bring us to salvation as well. Consider the testimony of any believer as to how they came to know Christ, and the chain of events that unfolds to bring them to that point of decision is amazing and would have been unpredictable at the time. And God does not desert us at the point of accepting Christ into our lives, rather providence functions to continue the work of sanctification:

> This it does in two ways. First, by quickening and reviving dying convictions and troubles for sins. Souls, after their first awakening, are apt to lose the sense and impression of their first troubles for sin, but Providence is vigilant to prevent it, and effectually prevents it. Secondly, Providence gives great assistance to the work of the Spirit upon the soul, by ordering, supporting, relieving and cheering means, to prop up and comfort the soul when it is over-burdened and ready to sink in the depths of troubles.

God's providence works in our lives to make us aware of our sin so that we will keep seeking after holiness instead of becoming satisfied with where we are at today in our lives. In addition, providence provides a 'barrier' and a 'hindrance to' sin entering into our lives. This is always important but even more so in the midst of a struggle or problem that is already overwhelming in and of itself. What is to prevent our sinful nature from breaking 'forth like an overflowing flood' to bring our own sin into a struggle which may not initially be reflective of any sin upon our part? How does providence help us in this particular struggle with sin?

> SOMETIMES by stirring up others to interpose with seasonable counsels, which effectually dissuade them from prosecuting an evil design. Thus Abigail meets David in the nick of time, and dissuades him from his evil purpose (1 Sam. 25:23–4).

This stresses the need for a counselor to be diligent and willing to be direct in their direction to the counselee. It may be that the sinful heart has entered into the person's struggle in a way that they are currently oblivious to. It is no comfort to them to avoid pointing out the danger of the temptation (if it is ready to burst forth) or the actual sin now entering into their life. Rather, the counselor may be a part of the providence of God to help prevent the occurring of the sin with its resulting destructive consequences. Yes, the person may already be hurting greatly so any confrontation needs to be gentle, 'not breaking the bruised reed' (Isa. 42:3), nonetheless it must be made so as to achieve the ends of providence.

Struggling people are by the nature of their struggles, seeing life in a more limited fashion, much like the horse going down the street with blinders on its eyes. The blinders help to keep the horse focused in the forward direction and not distracted by all the noise and confusion going on around it. We are much like those horses except the blinders prevent us from seeing the important bigger picture around us. We do glimpse things happening all around us, we have feelings churning inside and we struggle to focus on what it means to move forward. In the midst of the confusion and struggle, the sin nature is ready to pounce upon our own weakness and exert itself. 'Go, get drunk and you will feel better.' 'Leave your spouse and you will find someone who loves you more and makes you feel better.' 'Forget everyone else and love yourself for awhile.' 'End your life and the struggle will be over.' These thoughts are not sinful in and of themselves (they reflect temptation, not necessarily sin) but without help to stay focused on growth, they may well take control and lead the person off into sin that had not initially been present. The wise counselor recognizes this potential and seeks to head it off with preventative direction. In doing so, they become part of the work of providence in the struggler's life.

> Sometimes by laying some strong affliction upon the body, to prevent a worse evil. Thus Basil [one of the early Church fathers] was a long time exercised with a violent headache which he observed was used by Providence to prevent lust. Paul had

a thorn in the flesh, a messenger of Satan sent to buffet him, and this affliction, whatever it was, was ordained to prevent pride in him (2 Cor. 12:7).

This is a largely misunderstood and certainly disliked teaching of Scripture today – that God uses suffering at times to prevent us from being faced with temptations to which we would succumb. Suffering in the modern church is typically seen as clearly evil in nature. In one sense this is true since all suffering is a result of the Fall into sin, but it misses the truth that providence uses all suffering to our ultimate, eternal good and sometimes may even bring the suffering as a means of helping us in our spiritual growth. Suffering is never something to just be endured in a stoic, grit your teeth, I can handle this type of manner. Rather, it is to be seen as a result of being in a sinful world, yet as something that God will use to help us in our own inner battle to overcome the sinful nature. We can truly mourn with those who struggle while also encouraging them to seek to find not their own strength, but God's strength to continue through the suffering.

> SOMETIMES sin is prevented in the saints by the better information of their minds at the sacred oracles of God. Thus, when sinful motions began to rise in Asaph's mind, from the prosperity of the wicked and his own afflicted state, and flew to such a height that he began to think all he had in the way of religion was little better than lost labor, he is set right again, and the temptation dissolved, by going into the sanctuary, where God showed him how to take new measures of persons and things, to judge them by their ends and issues, not the present appearances (Ps. 73:12–17).

Asaph actually 'increased his depression by trying to understand all the intricacies of God's ways; the same can be true for us.' That is, as he tried to come up with an answer to the question of why the wicked were healthy and prosperous and he was not, he found himself sliding further and further into a despairing state in which he almost walked away from his faith in God. The goal is not to ignore the reality of the question, nor is it to avoid struggling with the question, but it is to recognize we may not be able to come to a complete answer to the question and we must always ask these questions in a way that keeps us seeking or holding onto God. We can hold onto God and believe he truly cares even if we do not completely understand his answers back to us. This is the attitude of Asaph and the other Psalm writers as they struggle with these questions, as versus the grumblers in the wilderness who turned their backs upon God and suffered judgment (Num. 11).

'MEDITATION ON THE PROVIDENCE OF GOD'

Having established the existence of providence, Flavel builds upon the idea of intentionally reflecting upon the working of providence in the world to now 'prove it to be the duty of the people of God to meditate upon these performances of providence for them, at all times, but especially in times of difficulty and trouble.' This is our duty, he says, because God has commanded it (Jer. 7:12, Micah 6:5) and Scripture everywhere condemns the neglect of it as a sin (Isa. 26:11; 5:12–13; Ps. 28:4–5). 'And for this end and purpose it is that the Holy Ghost has affixed notes of attention such as "behold" to the narratives of the works of Providence in Scripture.' I must personally confess never having thought of the 'beholds' of Scripture in this way before reading Flavel! But his point is well made, that God does distinctly draw the attention of believers to his works in order that we will note them and remember them. Unfortunately, the typical response of people is only to note them in the present – to be glad and thankful at the time of a special deliverance – but then forget it shortly thereafter. One cannot read the Old Testament history of Israel without realizing that miraculous works of God rarely result in lasting faith. They produce a short term response that typically fades over time. The whole terrible saga of the Book of Judges illustrates this point too well as do the histories of Kings and the relevant prophetic writings. Even in the short earthly life of Christ, the initial response and then forgetting by the time of the crucifixion are amazing to consider. I suspect we tend to think we would not have run away at the arrest of Christ, and yet in struggle and suffering we too tend to forget the past providences of God. Each time I complain, whether about health, lack of finances, lack of respect, or whatever comes to mind, I am indicating a failure to remember and apply the past providences of God to my life today. For he did everything for me at the cross and has been willing to bless from that point on as well. These works of God are vitally important to remember, 'all these invite and call men to a due and deep observation of them.'

God clearly calls upon us to remember his works of redemption (Exod. 12, 1 Cor. 11:17f, Lord's Supper). These memorials are 'the food our faith lives upon in days of distress (Ps. 74:14). From Providences past saints argue to fresh and new ones to come.' So David; 'The Lord who delivered me from the paw of the lion and the paw of the bear will deliver me from the hand of this Philistine' (1 Sam. 17:37). 'Do you still not understand? Don't you remember the five loaves for the five thousand, and how many basketfuls you gathered?' (Matt. 16:9). And yet, like ancient Israel, our more typical response is to not remember, let alone consider how those past workings of God relate to my current struggles. Interestingly, the subject of the past is considered an important part of counseling practice, although there is debate about the methodology and purpose for examining and discussing a person's past in the counseling session. Without entering into that particular discussion, Flavel points us to at least one crucial reason for considering a person's past – to help them reflect upon God's providences to them from their birth to their conversion to all the other small and large ways in which God has worked in their lives. Of course, we should not limit their reflections to just their own lives as that runs the danger of becoming self-focused. We should also encourage reflecting upon Scriptural events (Abraham, Joseph, Mary, Christ, Paul and so many others) and upon the history of God's church (hence Flavel's reference earlier to the early church father Basil). Today, our philosophical and methodological direction seems to be centered on today, yesterday does not matter, traditions and historical understandings are unimportant, perhaps even dangerously limiting and constrictive. Flavel argues against all of this – historical understanding and reflection upon God's working is important, not just for apologetics (to defend the faith as being true) but even more so for the practical work of spiritual growth to occur in our lives, especially for those times of distress that everyone experiences somewhere during their life journey.

Lest we fall into another modern day trap, Flavel has a warning. He states that 'in all Providences, especially in some, he comes near to us. He does so in his judgments: "I will come near to you for judgment" (Mal. 3:5). He comes near in mercies also, "The Lord is near to all who call on him (Ps. 145:18)."' Too often we think of God's providence as indicating that no harm will come to us, we will not suffer in any manner. Flavel counters this by recognizing that God in his providence may discipline believers (Heb. 12:4–13) to help us overcome or even avoid falling into sin as well as mercifully deliver and assist us through trials (1 Cor. 10:13). Too often believers today think of providence only in terms of protection and being lifted up out of their hurts or struggles. As a result, they fail to discern the hand of providence when it brings discipline upon sin or discipline in the sense of the disciple, learning to trust God in the dark, mysterious times when his presence is not so obvious to us. A recent conversation with a missionary candidate brings this to mind. Having come back from a short-term trip to her eventual field of service, she expressed having struggled with fear after waking up in the middle of the night thinking someone was in the room to hurt her. As she struggled with this upon her return to the U.S. she related how she had often struggled with the fear of being hurt in the past. On her own she came to the understanding of how she was involved in idolatry as she was living as if she should and could protect herself when in reality only God could, so she needed to trust him alone for protection. I commended her for this excellent insight into the basis of the fear but asked her to add one qualifying thought to the process – to recognize that God may not necessarily physically protect her in this world but he has her totally protected for the next (Rom. 8:38–9). This is to see his providential care now (which she was seeing and relating) but also recognize that he has an eternal purpose in our lives, not just a short-term one and so we must understand what his 'deliverance' means and does not mean in any given situation.

How should we go about trying to reflect upon the providences of God? In a truly pastoral fashion, Flavel does not just state the doctrine and the need of it but also proceeds to help his congregation understand how to reflect upon God's providences in a way that does bring faith in the immediate trial. He urges them to labor diligently to recognize the acts of providence around them, and then reflect upon them fully, 'extensively and intensively. Let them be as extensively full as may be. Search backward into all the performances of providence throughout all your lives (see Asaph, Ps. 77:11–12).' If we take the time to truly reflect on what God has already done in our lives then 'if your hearts do not melt before you have gone half through that history, they are hard hearts indeed.'

So let the reflection process be extensive, look at our entire lives and look fully at them to see how God was acting, not coincidence or chance, but God's providential hand. Our typical tendency is to be selective and narrowly focused as we look at the past and present or even the future in the case of those struggling with fear and anxiety (those horse blinders again!). Rather, we need to cast our view back through all of our life and look in all directions. I can remember an instance of this in my past as a prison chaplain. I reached a point where I felt the ministry was pointless, there seemed to be no lasting fruit and so I was discouraged about even continuing to try. God led me into an exercise in what I now realize was a reflection upon his providence. I felt challenged by God to write down any incident of ministry no matter how trivial it seemed. When I first looked at the list, I offered protests. I noted a case in which I came in the middle of the night to talk to a suicidal inmate and here two years later he was still alive and had not thought about suicide again. But he had not accepted Christ was my protest. God's answer was simple – a dead man can not accept Christ, so it was effective ministry, even if not yet completed ministry. Similarly, I thought of a correctional officer who had left his wife. I was allowed to intervene and the marriage was restored, but again I protested because he was not strongly committed to the Lord (and at the time of writing this years later he is actually professing a different religious belief!) but again God reminded me that the restoration of the marriage was a successful ministry event in and of itself even if not all that is to be desired. When we narrow our focus and definitions of God being at work, we bring about discouragement. Rather we need to meditate in an 'extensive' manner.

But Flavel also urges intensive meditation which he describes, 'do not let your thoughts swim like feathers upon the surface of the waters, but sink like lead to the bottom.' In our 'microwave' culture we are usually in a hurry and this is true of counseling struggles as well. Everyone wants a quick, fast solution to whatever their struggle may be (and personally I am sensitive to that desire as I feel it myself both as a counselor and as a fellow struggler) but here Flavel points us to the value of long and perhaps even labored reflection upon God's work and seeking repeatedly to see how he is working now instead of assuming from one or two quick 'glances' that he is not at work and has abandoned the person in their struggle to fend for themselves. Patience trials are obviously difficult but as one who practices 'microwave' cooking because it is so much easier, let me say that it never is as good or nutritious as those well thought out cooked from scratch meals by my wife! Counselors feel pressured by time, by the desires of those they seek to help, and in the professional realm by the constraints of fees and insurance restrictions, but we must challenge those we help to see that patience and depth of reflection are key to counseling effectiveness that will continue for years to come rather than for only weeks or months.

There can be danger in reflecting upon our experiences as has too often occurred. People at times raise their experiences and their understanding of them to the level of biblical authority. While encouraging a reflection upon experiences, Flavel balances this with the warning of where ultimate authority lies. 'In all your observations of providence have special respect to that Word of God which is fulfilled and made good to you by them. This is a clear truth that all providences have relation to the written Word (1 Kings 8:24).' Providential acts by themselves are far from a perfect guide as we do not always understand the twists and turns of God's works. But as we bring them to the Scripture, they begin to take on clearer meaning as noted in Psalm 73:17, 'Until I entered the sanctuary of God; then I understood their final destiny.'

We sometimes speak of 'introspection' in which the person seems to be lost in their own reflections into themselves. Reflection upon God's providential works is quite different. It does entail understanding how I feel or think about what I see of God's work but its focus is not primarily internal, rather it involves an internal reflection in order to push me back to a reflection outward or upwards to God and how he is trying to guide me now. Introspection makes the internal reflection and finding solutions internally the answer and so ends up producing even more problems for the struggler as it is based solely on their own self.

Flavel brings forth several cautions on how to prevent abusing providence in our lives.

> If Providence delays the performance of any mercy to you that you have long waited and prayed for, yet see that you do not despond, nor grow weary of waiting upon God for that reason. First, the delay of your mercies is really for your advantage. You read, "yet the Lord longs to be gracious to you" (Isa. 30:18). What is that? Why, it is nothing else but the time of his preparation of mercies for you, and your hearts for mercy, that so you may have it with the greatest advantage of comfort. The foolish child would pluck the apple while it is green; but when it is ripe, it drops of its own accord and is more pleasant and wholesome.

I can personally understand this wonderful illustration. We have raspberries in our yard and I love to eat them every year (to the point where admittedly selfishness creeps in, not wanting to share them with others!). So as soon as they begin to ripen I'm ready to pick them and sometimes I pick them red but not quite red enough. They are still good but usually need some sugar to help them out, but when I wait and pick that really ripe, red raspberry it is simply wonderful right off the vine. So too with the providences of God in the right time determined by him, whereas we tend to seek too early before the mercy is 'ripe.' Again, the idea of patience and time enters into the counseling growth process. Urging people to grow quickly may be necessary in the sense of avoiding ongoing destructive consequences of their behavior, as in the person who is struggling with lashing out at others with anger. But at the same time, we have to encourage them to stay focused on the truth that God's work in their lives may take time to come to its complete fruition and so they need to be prepared to persevere through failures to ultimate growth. Marriage and family counseling is fraught with this dilemma – more than one person is involved so the time to bring about change from years of mistakes and dysfunction does not occur overnight. It may take months or even years of persevering in doing what the person knows to be right, regardless of outward results. In time the fruit will be ripe and truly taste good, but they must trust God with that process, and focus daily on how they should perform in order to love God and love others, specifically in their family situation.

'Consider that the mercies you wait for are the fruits of pure grace. You do not deserve them, nor can claim them upon any title of desert; and therefore have reason to wait for them in a patient and thankful frame.' This last point is prevalent in our lives. Too often I find myself claiming, usually not openly but deeply in the motives of heart, that I deserve God to act in such and such a way, perhaps because I feel I personally deserve it or at least because others are doing better than I am, and I am certainly as faithful as they are! Counselees easily fall into this trap as well. But the truth is that we received totally undeserved grace through the Cross of Christ and although God does accept as his children all who trust in Christ, we still deserve nothing. Christ is the worthy one who deserved glory and majesty but gave that up to die the miserable death upon the cross that we deserved. Now we live with his righteousness in our lives, but that makes us no more deserving than before, simply forgiven, justified, and accepted by God as his children because of Christ.

Similar to this is Flavel's final warning that we tend to want to explain everything so we can have certainty about what God is or is not doing in our lives. He cautions us not to 'pry too curiously into the secrets of providence nor allow your shallow reason arrogantly to judge and censure its designs.' We must take care to understand that as with Joseph in Genesis or Asaph in Psalm 73 the meaning of providential acts may be unclear to us at the time, only to be made clear later in our lives, or in some cases not until eternity.

ADVANTAGES OF MEDITATING UPON PROVIDENCE

Sleeplessness is a well-known struggle for many depressed and anxious people. Flavel provides a difficult but needed corrective on this struggle. He challenges us to move aside from the hurry and obsessions of our lives, 'to sit alone and think on these things, and press these marvelous manifestations of God in his providences upon our own hearts.' If we do this, then we will find that these meditations will force themselves into the depth of our being. Then we will experience the Psalmist's words (Psalm 4:8), 'I will lie down and sleep in peace, for you alone, O Lord, make me dwell in safety.' The Psalmist is stating that he will not allow the fear of life's events to rob him 'of his inward quiet, nor torture his thoughts with anxious forebodings.' As we grasp more and more that God is in control we are able to release problems to his care instead of obsessing upon them as if our constant rehearsing of them in our minds will somehow bring them under our control at last. It may require a constant struggle to develop this as a discipline but it is certainly worth entering that struggle. I can remember times of challenging people to write down their obsessive anxiety on a piece of paper, promising themselves to return to it later but for now leaving it in God's hands. This simple technique does not always work but it has helped a person at times to focus upon some other necessary task or even to sleep. When they return to the thought it may seem as overwhelming as before but they are already on their way, albeit slowly, to learning how to commit to God that which we have no control over.

Flavel continues by noting that there are several things in providence that bring the Christian's mind to this point of peace in strife. First is the 'supremacy of Providence and its uncontrollable power in working.' That is, God is all-powerful and will accomplish his purposes, nothing in creation can stop him. That being so, we have a peace knowing that he is in control and his providence is at work, so the dictator or the evil person or the corrupt government are not ultimately in control of my life – God is. Second is the 'profound wisdom of providence in all that it performs for the people of God.' The wheels are full of eyes (Ezek. 1:18), that is, there is an intelligent and wise Spirit that sits upon and governs the affairs of this world.' God is not only all-powerful but also all-knowing and all-wise. And finally Flavel points out God's care for us while we were still enemies of God, how He bestowed mercies to us and brought us to himself, before we even knew we were seeking to find him! One is reminded here of the life of John Newton, author of the hymn Amazing Grace, and how God brought him through years of immorality, near death, and direct participation in the slave trade to eventually become a preacher of the gospel and an instrumental force in helping William Wilberforce lead the campaign that eventually banished slavery in the British Empire.

APPLICATION OF THE DOCTRINE OF PROVIDENCE

In many ways, Flavel has already applied the doctrine of providence as he has been writing, which may explain why this section is actually the shortest of the three. It becomes more of his summary section encouraging his readers once again to the important necessity of not just living in the works of providence, but actively considering and reflecting upon them in their lives. 'If, as we have seen, God performs all things for you, God is to be owned by you in all that befalls you in this world, whether it is in a way of success and comfort, or of trouble and affliction.'

Providence has wide application to daily life. Flavel made references to prayer and providence, and now he notes the relationship between providence and that often asked question, what is God's will for me in this situation? His rules for our search after God's will state –

~ First, we should genuinely fear God, 'be really afraid of offending him. God will not hide his mind from such a soul (Ps. 25:14).'
~ Secondly, study Scripture more and the concerns of this world less.
~ Third, take what we know and practice it in daily life (John 7:17).
~ Fourthly, pray for God's guidance in our walk (Ezra 8:21).

~ Finally, 'follow providence so far as it agrees with the Word and no further.'

Flavel's emphasis reminds us of the danger of Christians seeking to discover God's guidance without utilizing Scripture. Too many today seek God's guidance through personal feelings, 'special' experiences of God, 'secret' knowledge, and so on but God's guidance is based upon and comes through his revealed Word.

Practically, Flavel captures in his final short chapter, one of the modern counseling tools often utilized to help people in their struggles – the idea of keeping a diary. But Flavel sees it as much more than its typical usage in counseling. He specifically encourages that we record the 'experiences of Providence' in our lives.

> What an antidote would it be to their souls against the spreading atheism of these days, and satisfy them beyond what many other arguments can do, that 'The Lord – he is God! The Lord – he is God!' (1 Kings 18:39). Written memorials secure us against that hazard, and besides, make them useful to others when we are gone, so that you do not carry away all your treasure to heaven with you, but leave these choice legacies to your surviving friends.

I can think of no more appropriate way to close this chapter than by noting the comments of Sinclair Ferguson, for me a modern example of the Puritan pastor. Ferguson is a theologian, an academic, and yet also a Pastor who brings deep truths to others in understandable ways so that they might grow thereby. To him I owe the debt of a lecture on *The Mystery of Providence* which led me to read this ever timely book for myself. In his summary of the applications of the book, Ferguson spells out loudly and clearly a number of biblical principles which Christians today desperately need to hear and which are directly relevant to any ministry of counseling:

~ God is in control of his universe.
~ God is working out his perfect purposes.
~ God is not my servant.
~ God's ways are far more mysterious and wonderful than I can understand.
~ God is good – all of the time; I can trust him – all of the time.

- God's timetable is not the same as mine.
- God is far more interested in what I become than in what I do.
- Freedom from suffering is not part of the promise of the Christian gospel.
- Suffering is an integral part of the Christian life.
- God works through suffering to fulfill his purpose in me.
- God's purposes, not mine, are what bring him glory.
- God guides me by enabling me to read his Providences through the lens of his Word.
- I have few greater pleasures than tracking the wonders of God's ways.[6]

6 Ferguson, 'The Mystery of Providence' in *The Devoted Life – An Invitation to the Puritan Classics* (Downers Grove: InterVarsity Press, 2004), 222–3.

3

ANXIOUS AND DISSATISFIED –
CONTENTMENT IS THE CURE[1]

In the modern world there exists a common sense of personal and even communal restlessness, discontent, fear, and even despair at the thought of another day, let alone tomorrow. What has become noticeably absent in the lives of many Christians (and non-Christians as well) is any realization or understanding of the concept of contentment. The majority of people have known times of relative peace or happiness but a deep abiding sense of contentment escapes most today on any consistent basis in their lives. In the context of counseling this becomes more obvious as people struggle with marriages that do not bring the satisfaction they had dreamed of, or face the ravages of tragedy and grief that bring into question the very purpose and value of living in this world. Even for believers who know Christ as their Savior, there is a struggle to find a foundation or anchor to settle themselves upon during difficulties and during times of seeming boredom and lack of excitement. Knowing Christ

---

1 All quotations in this chapter are from Jeremiah Burroughs, *The Rare Jewel of Christian Contentment*, Banner of Truth Trust edition, 2005 reprint, unless otherwise indicated.

does not automatically result in finding contentment based upon that knowledge and commitment in the personal life.

Jeremiah Burroughs (1599–1646) experienced these turmoils in his own life's journey as well as with those he served as a teaching pastor. After his graduation from Cambridge he was forced to flee to Rotterdam, Holland to avoid the persecutions during the reign of Charles I and the Laudian persecution directed towards the nonconformist pastors. While there he served as the teaching pastor for the English congregation for four years, where he taught along with William Bridge (see Chapter Six). Following his time of exile, he was able to return to England during the reforms brought about by the Long Parliament and became the 'Gospel preacher' in the congregations of Stepney and Cripplegate, both in London. He was also called upon to participate in the Westminster Assembly of the Divines although he died before the work was completed. As a pastor during times of persecution, he understood personally and pastorally the struggles that people experience and the questions that arise as they face an uncertain and dangerous future. Participating in exile brought this truth home more directly as he experienced the uprooting coupled with the longing for return to your own country and people. And all the time in exile, while serving those you are with, you feel concern for those still at home whom you hoped to see becoming free to worship God and growing in their spiritual lives apart from the theological battles of the day. Burroughs is uniquely placed to speak on the subject of contentment as his was certainly a life laced with turmoil and uncertainty. *The Rare Jewel of Christian Contentment* represents sermons gathered together and published two years after his early death. For the modern reader, they are a gem, representing the practical applications of a pastor-theologian who had experienced tumultuous times with his flock and led them through to Christian maturity.

'Contentment in every condition is a great art, a spiritual mystery. It is to be learned, and to be learned as a mystery.' So begins Burroughs' advice to fellow believers. There is a mystery about contentment just as there is about faith. While we know and believe in God and his existence we can not absolutely prove that existence and so faith becomes our bulwark, believing in that which can not be seen or touched, 'being sure of what we hope for and certain of what we do not see' (Heb. 11:1). Contentment is something to be learned, experienced and practiced, an 'art.' It does not automatically occur in the believer's life upon conversion and most commonly the experience of trials and sinful failures provide the opportunities to learn the art of finding contentment. In Western Christianity, those who are struggling are too often looking for quick solutions, ten steps to victory, explanations or even labels for their problems, all with the goal of finding quick relief. Contentment can be found in Christ but as an art it must be experienced, learned, and utilized in those struggles as a larger goal beyond the relief of the struggle itself.

The emphasis on mystery helps to push us back to how God works and away from the more mechanistic (follow the ten logical steps!) approaches that we try to devise for solving problems. James Payton, Jr. notes that while all Christian traditions do affirm the concept of mystery, modern day evangelicalism tends to treat mystery as "something to be solved," in contrast to the Orthodox Church where "mystery is to be celebrated, not solved. In Orthodoxy, mystery leads to wonder, silence and praise – not to explanation."[2]

This is not to say that we should not seek knowledge and wisdom about contentment which Burroughs himself will provide throughout the remainder of his book. But at the outset we must guard against trying to reduce finding contentment to formulaic understandings or to some simple 1-2-3 process for finding peace in our daily lives. The Lament Psalms (examples – Psalm 3, 10, 13 and many others) are indicative of this process as the authors express their distress and even doubt God's work in their lives. But through those doubts they are able to seek and find God at an even deeper level in their Christian experience. It is something to be learned, and not just once, it is part of the ongoing learning process in the life of the believer (note David's repeated lament Psalms on the same subject of whether God was protecting him from his enemies or not – not just one Psalm but repeated times David has to struggle with this doubt in his life).

2 James R. Payton, Jr., Interview, *IVP Academic Alert*, vol. 16, no. 2, Spring 2007, 3.

And it is a mystery too. Again the Lament Psalms illustrate this well. Often in counseling situations I direct individuals to the Lament Psalms as an example of how to struggle through their doubt, anger, or despair with God in a 'brutally honest manner.' They read a few of the Psalms and then ask the inevitable question, 'Ok, what do I do first, what is the first step?' Of course, these Psalms do not reduce to steps (a phenomena of modern popular counseling and psychology books which typically try to reduce complex processes to simple easy steps, which usually do not work). The answer is always the same, there are no direct steps, study what David or Asaph is doing, and model your relationship with God upon that process.[3] This reflects the element of mystery that Burroughs (and Orthodox theology) is referring too. We can see what God is doing, see who he is and even understand to some degree because he has revealed himself to us through his Word and through Christ. But we do not fully know and so the element of mystery is left for us. Contentment is part of that mystery. How can someone be content in the midst of the worst situations – we can illustrate it from Scripture such as Paul in prison, 'I have learned to be content whatever the circumstances' (Phil. 4:11), but we can never fully explain it for it is a work of God in the person's life, not simply a set of beliefs or rules of conduct that they follow.

CONTENTMENT DESCRIBED

> I OFFER the following description: Christian contentment is that sweet, inward, quiet, gracious frame of spirit, which freely submits to and delights in God's wise and fatherly disposal in every condition.... Not only must the tongue hold its peace; the soul must be silent. Many may sit silently, refraining from discontented expressions, yet inwardly they are bursting with discontent.

Wisely, Burroughs shies away from trying to define contentment, instead seeking to describe the indications and attitudes evident

---

3 I am indebted for these insights to Dr. Tremper Longman, III from his lectures and *The Cry of the Soul*, written with Dan Allender. See also Michael Card's *a Sacred Sorrow*.

in one who is experiencing contentment before God. Immediately developing a strong emphasis in his book, he points away from outer behaviors and into the heart, the inner person, for the place where contentment is found or is absent. Many believers have determined how to express outward contentment – 'I am satisfied with God and trust him that he knows best in this current tragedy in my life' – while inwardly they are struggling against that which they express outwardly. Too often they have been unwittingly seduced to follow a stoic approach to life, which presents an outward sense of acceptance and calm, while internally they are experiencing turmoil that they fear to express. The too common refrain that Christians are not depressed or anxious or angry easily leads to outward stoicism and internal turmoil as people struggle to maintain the image of the 'together' believer for others to see. As a philosophy, stoicism has actually become quite common in evangelical church teaching without a realization that it is being taught and practiced.

Many of those in counseling settings feel they are failing because they are unable to 'just suck it up and get on with life.' In following this approach the inner turmoil is left unattended and they actually miss the opportunity for growth that the situation is presenting to them, to help them learn true contentment in the midst of trial. I find myself reminding people constantly that although they do not want the struggle they are engaged in and I would not want it in my life either, they actually have a unique opportunity from the Lord that other believers may not be experiencing. They have come to the point in their struggle where they realize they are not in control and they can not overcome it on their own so they know they must turn to God. Many other believers are going blithely on their way not realizing that they are trusting in their own strength and wisdom and sense of control of the situations around them. The one struggling is no longer self-deceived, they are presented with the opportunity to more deeply understand themselves and by so doing be led to a deeper understanding of and dependence upon God. It may not be a choice they wished for but the lack of inner biblical contentment is a worse fate as it represents in Burroughs' strong words, 'a perverse disorder' which is often hidden from the view of the person and others around them.

> CONTENTMENT is the quiet of the heart. It is not opposed to making in an orderly manner our moans and complaints to God, and to our friends. Though a Christian ought to be quiet under God's correcting hand, he may without any breach of Christian contentment come plain to God... Likewise he may communicate his sad condition to his Christian friends, showing them how God has dealt with him, and how heavy the affliction is upon him, that they may speak a word in season to his weary soul.

For Burroughs, the Lament Psalms or the Book of Job would function as illustrations of believers truly seeking to find contentment by expressing their doubts and complaints to God or even other believers, not simply to express them (this was part of the mistake of the grumblers in the wilderness who were judged for their complaining) but in order that they might hold onto their belief in God while seeking to hear him speak into their doubts and struggles. This process of struggle does not inherently lead them away from the pursuit of contentment, rather it can be a crucial part of how they find contentment. Even Christ evidences this type of struggle in the Garden of Gethsemane (Matt. 26:36–46) when he asks of God, not once but three times, for another way than to drink the cup of wrath which will bring such physical, emotional, and spiritual suffering upon him. His contentment with God's will in his life is modeled not through an outward stoic acceptance but through a very human time of questioning with God as to the possibility of an alternative (easier!) way. Knowing there was no other way, he does proceed in contentment that the suffering is part of the plan of God to bring redemption to sinners through his sacrificial death, and that God will be with him in the time of suffering.

With this explanation it is still difficult to grasp what Burroughs is speaking of with his phrase 'quiet of the heart.' But he offers assistance by utilizing a typical Puritan form of preaching and writing, stating what is in opposition to being quiet in the heart or spirit. 'What, then, is this quietness of spirit opposed to? It is opposed to murmuring and repining at the hand of God.' Here he points us back once again to the difference between those who wrote laments in Scripture (David, Jeremiah, Job) and the grumblers during the wilderness wanderings whom God chose to destroy. The major differences seem to be that with the lamenters, while they may state their complaint as a statement before God, it is as if they actually have a question mark at the end of the statement, as in 'God you are not faithful?' as versus the grumblers who make statements with exclamation marks at the end, 'God, you are not faithful!' In the first, there is doubt, confusion, perhaps even anger but still a sense that God will somehow respond and help with the conflicting emotions. In other words they are being 'brutally honest' but sincerely seeking God. In the second, there is no expectation that God will speak and actually no real desire to hear him speak, they have a settled opinion already, a 'do not confuse me with the facts' type of approach. The second major difference is that the lamenters are distinctly approaching God with their struggles, whereas the grumblers are not really addressing God at all but making statements about God to others around them. So the grumblers are in Burroughs' words, 'murmuring' against God, rather than honestly seeking to speak with God.

Secondly, 'quiet of the heart' is opposed to 'vexing and fretting, which is a degree beyond murmuring.' Here Burroughs recognizes the anxious, fearful heart which is more like the pagans than the believers, 'for the pagans run after all these things, and your heavenly Father knows that you need them' (Matt. 6:32). In writing about anxiety, Matthew understands the way that unbelievers are obsessed with food, clothing, and shelter as they 'run' through their daily lives trying to find security in these areas. It reminds one of the cliché about having to 'climb the ladder of success' only to find out it is a 'treadmill.' Matthew's challenge to believers is to avoid the way of paganism and demonstrate trust in God who will provide all that is needed in his own way and time. Burroughs too recognizes that anxiety at its core reflects a lack of contentment that is willing to trust God in the absence of current physical evidence of his working. Anxiety, worry, or fear can be complicated in its appearance in people's lives but underneath the outward specifics lies a core of feeling that God can not be fully trusted, rather the person has to be engaged in various behaviors or in worrying and obsessing in order to be certain that things will work out. Of course, their anxiety does not produce results and so it feeds upon itself and brings increased anxiety leading to a downward spiral in the person's life. The beginning for Burroughs would be to recognize that this reflects a struggle with truly exercising faith in God and being content with whatever he allows to occur in our lives.

Thirdly, 'quiet of the heart' is opposed 'to tumultuousness of spirit, when the thoughts run distractingly and work in a confused manner.' Those seeking contentment may have many emotions struggling together (as in the biblical Laments) but they are focused on seeking direction and comfort in God, rather than being scattered everywhere searching in all the wrong places for contentment and peace.

Fourthly, it is opposed 'to an unsettled and unstable spirit, whereby the heart is distracted from the present duty that God requires in our several relationships, towards God, ourselves and others.' Returning again to Matthew 6, this time verse 33, 'seek first his Kingdom and his righteousness, and all these things [food, clothing, shelter] will be given to you as well.' Contentment does not necessarily have all the answers, nor does it reflect a complete lack of internal struggle or emotions, but it is unswerving in moving ahead to serve God and advance his Kingdom even as it continues to struggle, instead of allowing those difficulties to distract the individual to pursuing self-focused solutions. So, even as a spouse may be considering divorce, the other spouse must seek to biblically love them, rather than spouting off promises to do this or that, or seeking vacations, special gifts, or trying to bring a child into their lives in hopes of saving the marriage.

Fifthly, it is 'opposed to distracting, heart-consuming cares.' Instead of focusing upon our fears and cares, contentment seeks to focus on the greatness of God's power, mercy and grace. Do we know how he will respond in our situation? No. But do we know who he is from the history of his working in Scripture? Yes. Contentment seeks to move away from the daily cares and worries to focus on the God of Scripture in his past work and his future promises. This is one of the functions of the Lord's Supper as a memorial, to force us to take those few moments to reflect back once again on what God has done in the past, particularly the redemption achieved through the crucifixion and resurrection of Christ, as well as projecting us into the future where his promise is that the final fulfillment of the work of the cross in each believer's life will be accomplished upon their entrance into heaven. This and many other reflections in Scripture should be constant reminders to turn away from the cares and discouragements of day to day life to remember who God is in the midst of those very discouragements. How will he work in the midst of the person's specific struggles? We may not know the answer to that question but we know from his nature, his past acts, and his promises, that he will act according to their ultimate benefit. In addition, his promises state that nothing in all creation can separate us from his love (Rom. 8:28–39). No problem or struggle is greater than God and so no struggle can break our relationship established with him through the redemptive work of Christ on our behalf.

Sixthly, 'it is opposed to sinful shiftiness and shirking to get relief and help. We see this kind of thing in Saul running to the witch of Endor, and offering sacrifice before Samuel came.' Burroughs was well aware that people do not enjoy discontent, they seek to remove it by any means possible. The question is what means they use to accomplish this goal. King Saul attempted to remove his discontent – the fear of the upcoming battle's outcome – by seeking to know the future through the efforts of a fortune-teller witch. Today some use drugs, alcohol, or other idolatrous addictions to remove the feelings of discontent. Others may use relationships or job success or a host of other means to try to cover over the discontent that they feel. But this is in opposition to finding genuine contentment for it focuses them away from biblical directions to temporary 'fixes' that allow them to feel better without ever addressing the true inner turmoil that they feel. Our society of quick 'fixes' and relativistic values continues to provide impetus for this mad search for anything that promises contentment regardless of its ability to actually deliver on its promise. The advertising world alone illustrates this truth as they commonly appeal to the sense of discontent (or seek to create the sense!) in order to sell a product. Some of the products are genuinely worthwhile while many others are either unnecessary or even fraudulent (think of the host of diet pills that promise to burn off your fat without you doing anything different and you will then feel better about yourself). Contentment is not easily obtained and it is never obtained apart from seeking it through a relationship with God.

Finally, 'the last thing that quietness of spirit is the opposite of is desperate risings of the heart against God by way of rebellion.' This would represent the ultimate approach, to cast off any thought of contentment coming from a relationship to God, to instead reject him and seek to find contentment in your own strength and ways, that is to seek to become a god yourself.

In his initial description, Burroughs speaks of spiritual contentment as coming from 'the frame of the soul. The contentment of a man or woman who is rightly content does not come so much from outward arguments or from any outward help, as from the disposition of their own hearts. The disposition of their own hearts causes and brings growth to this gracious contentment rather than any external thing.' Contentment is not found in outward objects or pursuits, outward relationships, outward discussions. It is a matter of the inner person, the heart – whom do we trust in, what do we believe when faced with conflicts and doubts? Burroughs is not implying that others outside the person may not be used by God to help bring about inner contentment, after all that is the intent of his sermons (and of those who published them as the book) but he is stressing that contentment is an inner work that then reflects itself through the outer person.

Furthermore, if the contentment is truly present at the heart level, it will be demonstrated in the outer life of the person, not in just one incident or period of their life but as a habit, 'contentment is not merely one act, just a flash in a good mood. You find many men and women who, if they are in a good mood, will be very quiet. But this is not the constant tenor of their spirits to be holy and gracious under affliction.' He further notes that some people are naturally 'more still and quiet' in their constitution but this is not the same as contentment. Contentment is more than a personality trait, it is a spiritual condition of the heart that must be learned and grown in. And contentment is not just 'a sturdy resolution. Some men through the strength of a sturdy resolution do not seem to be troubled, come what may. So they are not disquieted as much as others.'

It is not, he notes, purely a rational ability to explain events and situations they may face and thereby find solace in their explanations. Outward contentment can be deceptive, it may not accurately reflect the inner heart of the person. In counseling settings the person who seems outwardly composed and together is often missed. Sometimes it is true that they are spiritually mature and have an inner foundation of trust and commitment. But at other times, they are simply reflecting these traits that Burroughs mentioned and need to be challenged to see the difference as reflected in true biblical contentment. Otherwise, they face a shallow spiritual existence, probably will offer shallow comfort and direction to others, and may well find themselves unprepared if an immense tragedy should come into their own life.

In typical Puritan fashion, Burroughs' initial description of contentment is still far from complete halfway through this chapter in his book. 'Freely submitting to and taking pleasure in God's disposal – It is a free work of the Spirit.' He explains four things concerning this freedom of the spirit:

> THAT the heart is readily brought over. When someone does a thing freely he does not need a lot of moving to get him to do it. Many men and women, when afflictions are come upon them, may be brought to a state of contentment with great ado. At last, perhaps, they may be brought to quiet their hearts in their affliction, but only with a great deal of trouble and not at all freely.

This points to the concept raised earlier, that being forced to accept the current condition is not equivalent to contentment. It is more of a passive state of compliance with something which the person feels they have no ability to change. Burroughs challenges this shallow spirituality – do not just passively accept what comes into your life, but actively choose to see it as a work that God would use to bring growth now and in the future. Looking at the life of Joseph in Genesis 37–50, it becomes clear that although Joseph knew God had a plan for his life, he walked much of the time in darkness, not understanding how that plan was working out. It was thirteen years from the time his brothers sold him as a slave until the time he was finally elevated to the position of the second most powerful person in the mighty kingdom of Egypt. But during that time the Scripture records how he actively served God and others (he is a wonderful example of love God and love others, Matt. 22:37–40) in whatever situation he found himself. In essence, he chose to accept the situations as given by God (substantiated later in his words to his brothers, Gen. 45:5–8 and 50:15–21).

> I⊤ is freely, that is, not by constraint. Not, as we say, patience by force. Thus many will say that you must be content: 'This is the hand of God and you cannot help it.' Oh, but this is too low an expression for Christians.

Do not just stoically accept the struggle but embrace the truth that God has a greater purpose in our lives and is himself greater than sin and struggle so that we can move beyond mere acceptance to rejoicing in our circumstances (consider again Joseph or Paul emphasizing rejoicing throughout the book of Philippians while in a Roman prison).

> THIS freedom is in opposition to mere stupidity. A man or woman may be contented merely from lack of sense. This is not free, any more than a man who is paralyzed in a deadly way and does not feel it when you nip him is patient freely.

Lack of understanding is not equivalent to contentment, it is simply that – a lack of understanding of what is truly happening. Lack of understanding may present outwardly as a spiritually mature behavior but would be deceptive. When helping those who struggle, this is another mistake made by counselors and other people helpers, to misinterpret outward actions as reflecting inner understanding. To do so, leaves the person at peril in the future for they may have simply followed instructions provided to them without understanding those instructions and thus developing the future foundation for weathering life's struggles with contentment. All of this is to say that in the final analysis contentment must reflect a choice made by the believer to submit to whatever God brings or allows in their lives, trusting in God's greater plan to work all things, including evil and tragedy, for ultimate good (Rom. 8:28–30). Forced contentment is much like court-ordered counseling, rarely of any lasting significance because the person does not embrace the truths at the heart level and seek to willingly make them their own, rather they feel coerced and respond only in order to mitigate or escape the current situation they face. The result is perhaps immediate, surface compliance but no long-term change or equipping to make different decisions in the future.

> CONTENTMENT is freely submitting to and taking pleasure in God's disposal. Perhaps some of you may say, like David, 'It is good that I was afflicted,' but you must come to this, 'It is good that I am afflicted.' Not just good when you see the good fruit it has wrought, but to say when you are afflicted, 'It is good that I am afflicted. Whatever the affliction, yet through the mercy of God mine is a good condition.'

Contentment is not truly present when everything is based upon looking back after we see God's actual work to then proclaim faith and trust and therefore contentment with him. Rather it is coming to the point where belief in God's goodness and providential hand can be expressed in the midst of the affliction, when it is hard to tell how and when God will actually act. This reflects the deep heart belief that represents true contentment. If everything is based upon evidence of what has been seen, then faith is no longer necessary and as Burroughs is at pains to demonstrate, contentment and faith are integrally linked. Without faith in a God who has absolutely proved himself already – faith exercised even if we do not see him clearly today – there will be no contentment. The fallen world is a crazy place with dangers, afflictions, diseases, disasters. At any given moment, it does appear crazy to be content and believe in a sovereign God. This is why Paul notes that the 'peace of God which transcends all understanding will guard your hearts and minds in Christ Jesus' (Phil. 4:7). It is a supernatural peace, not a 'natural' or 'normal' one based upon observable circumstances but one which comes from God himself to the believer's heart.

FINDING CONTENTMENT

'A Christian comes to contentment, not so much by getting rid of the burden that is on him, as by adding another burden to himself. For if you can get your heart to be more burdened with your sin, you will be less burdened with your afflictions.' Just when the reader thinks Burroughs will make things easy and provide a nice formulaic way to find contentment, he once again disappoints. But the disappointment is to persuade us to avoid false ways of convincing ourselves that we have found contentment, to instead lead us to the only contentment that will survive and buttress the many years of our lives. He recognizes that it truly is a crazy thought that contentment comes by adding burdens, rather than subtracting them! And adding burdens is the last thing someone in counseling would want to hear about. After all, the person has already come burdened, they are seeking relief, removal, or at least support with carrying their burden! But it is not by the humanistic, we are 'good people' approaches that people will find relief or more importantly growth. It is found by facing the deceptions of our hearts, one of those being the notion that we are basically good people who make mistakes now and then. By first seeing ourselves as sinners always in need of God's grace, we are enabled to find the strength and righteousness of Christ which will allow us to overcome sin, love the unlovely, and persevere in 'dissatisfying' situations. Without confronting this deceptive belief with the truth of who we are, contentment will never be achieved.

For example, an individual who constantly sees themselves as a victim will begin to exercise a passive acceptance of their situations and even to some degree a feeling that they are at peace in accepting 'their lot in life.' But this seeming peace is based on an understanding that they are a good person who does not deeply sin themselves. They may be truly victimized at times (which is tragic and worthy of being confronted) but the turning of their personal identity into that of a victim is not equivalent to contentment, it is a poor substitute. They will find themselves driven to begin experiencing victimization when it is not present in order to find a false peace with their lot in life or the 'cross they must carry.' Burroughs drives us instead to look not just at the outward circumstances and our responses to them, but to learn to understand who we are before God, sinners who are made saints in Christ, but in and because of his strength, not our own. By adding this burden of seeing ourselves not as good ourselves, but as only capable of good in Christ, our perception of all other burdens is changed.

Counselors committed to following Scripture have often been accused of simplistically reducing all of life's problems to sin. While there is a degree of truth in this accusation in the sense that counselors may not sufficiently 'listen' to the person (James 1:19) so as to truly understand their struggle before speaking, and counselors may also blur the distinctions between personally committed sin and wrestling with the results of being sinned against or living with the effects of a fallen world (having a loved one killed by a drunk driver or developing cancer through no direct fault of your own). But at least three important truths are always present in the life of any struggler relative to sin. First is that sin is always involved in their struggle. Without the fall into sin of Genesis 3 there would be no struggle in this world. It is the presence of sin, whether ours or others or the general decay brought about by sin in general that is in some way implicated in all struggles. Second, as Burroughs so correctly points out, we are all sinners and are always capable of sinful responses in the midst of difficulty. Capable does not indicate we will always sin, but the knowledge of our capability is one of the bulwarks towards resisting sinful reactions to hardship. And thirdly, where sin is present there is always a remedy. The 'good' thing about sin is that God has provided the remedy through Christ's death on the cross. For the believer, confession and repentance leads to forgiveness and cleansing from sin (1 John 1:9). So when personal sin is present there is always an effective response the person can take! Burroughs does not want us to fall into the trap of thinking that our contentment is based upon outward circumstances going well or upon the removal of the burdens we feel, rather it is based in our relationship to Christ and the greatest of burdens that he removed for us – the sin that separated us from personal relationship with God.

'The way of contentment to a carnal heart is only the removing of the affliction. O that it may be gone! "No," says a gracious heart, "God has taught me a way to be content though the affliction itself still continues." There is a power of grace to turn this affliction into good, it takes away the sting and poison of it.' This is one of the most significant truths communicated in counseling situations, the goal is not removal of your problem, rather it is that you experience God in a deeper way in the midst of your struggle and grow to be more in the image of Christ. This is well illustrated in 2 Corinthians 12:7–11 as Paul describes his struggle with God over a physical weakness that was hindering his ability to serve God. Three times he asks for its removal and three times God replies with a No. Finally, God notes that 'My grace is sufficient for you, for my power is made perfect in weakness.' That is, we are strong not when the affliction is removed but when we experience God's power in a meaningful way in the midst of the weakness. The experience of that power may bring actual removal of the weakness or in Paul's case it may bring the ability to continue to serve God effectively despite the weakness. It is rather natural for us to enter a counseling office or seek a friend's help by saying help me to remove this depression, or anxiety, or anger. But Burroughs is correct to point us to the deeper truth that finding contentment in God in the midst of the struggle is the key, not a simple removal of the problem being experienced. The desire for removal reflects our tendency to want to avoid the hard work that is required for spiritual growth into maturity.

There are these circumstances that I am in, with my wants, I want this and this for comfort – well, how shall I come to be satisfied and content? A carnal heart thinks, I must have my wants made up or else it is impossible that I should be content. But a gracious heart says, 'What is the duty of the circumstances God has put me into?' Again the emphasis is not on meeting my definition of want, or perceived need, but instead focusing on what God states we require in this situation. One of the critical problems inherent in our psychologized culture today is the emphasis on 'I have to have my needs met' which does not distinguish between desires (which may be legitimate or not legitimate) and needs. Scriptures such as Matthew 6:33 unequivocally point to the truth that our only true 'need' is for God and the salvation he provides through Christ. Everything else is in the category of desires. God will provide us grace to deal with unmet desires, instead of the too common emphasis to push ahead and demand that my desires be met because they are being defined as needs. Many well-intentioned Christian counselors have encouraged people to demand that their needs be met by another person in the midst of counseling, instead of urging them to seek to love God first, others second, and practice self-denial relative to their own perceived needs. Burroughs anticipated this modern development by pointing to the fallacy of thinking contentment is found when my wants are being met. Contentment has nothing to do with my wants, rather it has to do with God supplying that which I truly need and which only he is the proper judge of. Contentment then seeks to push past unmet desires to trust God in the midst of those frustrated desires, seeking his strength to change our desires to more biblically legitimate ones and finding his strength to be content with legitimate desires left unmet this side of heaven.

> A gracious heart is contented by the melting of his will and desires into God's will and desires, by this means he gets contentment. The mystery consists not in bringing anything from outside to make my condition more comfortable, but in purging out something that is within. Jerome said, 'he is a happy man who when he is beaten, the stroke is a stroke of love.' All God's strokes are strokes of love and

mercy, all God's ways are mercy and truth, to those that fear him
and love him (Ps. 25:10).

Finding contentment starts and ends in our heart, not in the world or
people around us.

CHRIST AND CONTENTMENT

'A Christian finds satisfaction in every circumstance by getting
strength from another, by going out of himself to Jesus Christ, by his
faith acting upon Christ, and bringing the strength of Jesus Christ
into his own soul.' Much of today's Christianity has devolved into
moralism, in which we have the strength and ability to do what we
must do, so we set out to do it. While it may be truly moral in that the
goals are biblically valid, the source of ability is one that Scripture
would seriously question. It is not about conquering our anger
or problem with alcohol by utilizing our own strength, it is about
finding and depending upon Christ and his strength to overcome
it. While there may be relative success in our own strength at times
because our willpower is not totally corrupted by the Fall and so
is able to function properly at times to some degree, nonetheless
our strength does not bring the deep heart change that Burroughs
stresses. Rather, it is in finding God's strength in the midst of our
weakness that contentment can be achieved. Christ on earth was the
perfect illustration of this. He had more personal strength than any
of us as the perfect God-man, yet he constantly sought time alone
with God for strengthening, fellowship, and direction. In the Garden
of Gethsemane he did not adopt a John Wayne or 'Rambo' approach
to what was facing him and just go out to face it, gritting his teeth
and putting forth all his own strength. Rather, he wrestled with God
and ultimately was strengthened directly by God himself while the
human comforters he had hoped for were sound asleep!

Burroughs then points to specific lessons in the life of Christ that
aid us in our search for contentment. 'The lesson of self-denial....
That is the first lesson that Christ teaches any soul, self-denial,
which brings contentment, which brings down and softens a man's

heart.' Contentment does not come from seeking my purposes or my wants but from denying myself to instead seek to focus on loving God and loving others. The result will be that we learn we are truly nothing in ourselves (John 15:5). If we know we are nothing in the sense of deserving nothing, then we will be able to bear anything. 'Why should I make much of it, to be troubled and discontented if I have not got this and that, when the truth is that I can do nothing?' Furthermore, although God brings gifts and abilities into our lives, if he were then to leave us (which he promises not to do in the lives of believers) then those gifts and abilities would be empty and useless. To compound all this we still remain sinners, so that 'by sin we become a great deal worse than nothing. Sin makes us more vile than nothing, and contrary to all good!'

Contentment then comes when we turn from our own desires through self-denial to instead seek that which God desires to bring into our lives. It is desiring God himself, not our perceived comforts that will bring lasting contentment. 'Christ teaches you that there is vanity in all things in the world, and the soul which, by coming into the school of Christ, by understanding the glorious mysteries of the Gospel, comes to see the vanity of all things in the world, is the soul that comes to true contentment.'

Contentment is rooted in our perspective on ourselves and our circumstances. Rather than focusing upon ourselves (what we want, our feelings in our struggles) the challenge is to focus on Christ, 'who for the joy set before him endured the cross, scorning its shame, and sat down at the right hand of the throne of God' (Heb. 12:2). How did Christ endure the agony and literal torture of the crucifixion, he did not look at himself or his tormentors, rather he looked to the other side of the cross to the finished work of redemption and his restoration to relationship with his Father in Heaven. We tend to look inward or at our circumstances to find contentment but Burroughs reminds us that this world is vanity (or empty) and that which is of ourselves and not of God is vanity, it will fail and pass away. The secret for Christ was his focus upon seeking and living for the things that were truly of God. Christ challenged Martha to see that she was very busy about purposeful activities yet 'there is one thing necessary.' Like Martha we become busy in the service of God and miss God himself and so miss the source of contentment. We seek after wealth, health, pleasure, but what is truly necessary is that we have pardon for our sin, that we have a personal relationship with God, and that my soul should be saved by the redemptive work of Christ. It is in those areas that we find eternal contentment as versus the transient contentments we so often pursue.

Perhaps contentment's greatest struggle is that there is always something else missing that brings discontent! People pursue the wrong things to find contentment in life, and in the midst of struggle they often look for the wrong solutions – if only this had not happened, or if only I had married someone else, or if only I had more money. The source of contentment is not found in 'solutions' to all these scenarios but as Martha was instructed, it is found in knowing and following Christ wherever he might lead. God's created order was given to us to enjoy and use, but its value and pleasure is inherent in the Creator and not in the creation apart from its Creator. Burroughs is not against enjoyment (contrary to much negative writing against the Puritans, they did know how to enjoy the godly pleasures of this world, food being one example for many of them).

Finally, Christ teaches that to know contentment we must know the state of our own hearts. The Sermon on the Mount takes this direction by pushing us away from an emphasis on external sin back to the motivations of the heart which is where the sin is born before it reflects itself through behavioral actions. 'You must learn to know your own hearts well, to be good students of your own hearts. By studying your heart you will come soon to discover wherein your discontent lies.'

In other words, we have met the enemy and he is us! Discontent is a reflection of our heart's response to the difficulties of this world, not the unavoidable reaction to those difficulties. As such it reveals how we see and understand ourselves, our world, and our God. So, we must make reflection on the desires and motives of our hearts a key discipline to an effective life. Counselees too often focus only upon their immediate, surface struggle. We serve them well by helping them explore why their heart is responding to their struggles in the way it is. In a quite insightful recognition Burroughs notes that, 'by knowing their own hearts they know what they are able to manage. Now by knowing their hearts they know that they were not able to manage such prosperity.' And so they find contentment by not having something because they come to see they could not have properly handled it in their lives anyway! I have often joked with those I am ministering to that despite my plans on how I would wisely utilize a million dollars if God gave it to me, he must know my heart better than I because he has chosen not to so bless me! The truth behind this humor is that I recognize that God does know my heart better than I do, so I should learn to be content with what he has given to me, and use it wisely rather than create discontent by wishing for something more that I may not be able to ethically handle if I did have it.

EVIDENCES OF DISCONTENT

No Puritan work would be complete without evidences of the lack of the subject being discussed. Burroughs brings satisfaction in this area by discussing numerous evidences of a discontented heart. Among those he discusses are the 'evils of a murmuring spirit – by murmuring you undo your prayers, for it is exceedingly contrary to the prayers that you make to God.' Not content to leave it this general, he notes 'evil' effects from a murmuring rather than a contented spirit:

> BY murmuring and discontent in your hearts, you come to lose a great deal of time. How many times do men and women, when they are discontented, let their thoughts run and are musing and contriving, through their present discontentedness and let their discontent then work in them, for some hours together, and they spend their time in vain!

Here he is absolutely practical in his insights, how many of us have experienced this? Working on a project that just is not going well, frustration enters, we fret and grumble and by the time all is said and done, we have wasted large amounts of time spent in the grumbling or in the 'fixing' that has to occur because of our grumbling's lack of focus on just doing the job to the best of our ability to please God.

Anxiety strugglers consistently experience this, wasting time in their continued efforts to avoid the anxiety which do not really work and then feeling more anxious over the passage of time in which they can show little accomplished.

> IT unfits you for duty. If a man or woman is in a contented frame, you may turn such a one to anything at any time and he is fit to go to God at any time; but when one is in a discontented condition, that man or woman is exceedingly unfit for the service of God.

Discontent makes it extremely difficult to focus on loving God and loving others. Until the person is able to see contentment as rooted in their relationship to God and who he is, they find it hard to move ahead with instructions on how to work with their problems. And ministry duties become burdensome, adding to the discontent rather than bringing a sense of accomplishment at providing a useful service to others.

> UNTHANKFULNESS is an evil and a wicked effect which comes from discontent. The Scripture ranks unthankfulness among very great sins. Men and women, who are discontented, though they enjoy many mercies from God, yet they are thankful for none of them, for this is the vile nature of discontent, to lessen every mercy of God.

The history of Scripture demonstrates that we are quick to forget the past blessings of God to focus on the perceived 'failures' of God to deliver in the present. Throughout Israel's history they consistently 'forgot' what God had done and expected him to do more today to prove his faithfulness to them. And in a short period of time, Christ's crowd of supporters deserted him when he was arrested with only one of the twelve apostles being present at the crucifixion. One of the purposes of memorials throughout Scripture is to force us to stop, reflect, and remember who God is and what he has done so that we will be thankful in our present circumstances and with thankfulness comes contentment.

Burroughs moves from the evils that result from a discontented heart to the foolishness that is evident in the heart of discontent. '(1) It takes away the present comfort of what you have, because you have not something that you would have. What a foolish thing is this, that because I have not got what I want, I will not enjoy the comfort of what I have!' This is a common occurrence for those struggling with anxiety and depression. Their focus is upon the problems, the potential fears they have, so much so that they can not enjoy the life of today with the blessings it does bring. Perfectionists are so focused on having to establish their worth by achieving the ideal that they cannot find satisfaction in having done a job well, but not perfectly! '(2) By all your discontent you cannot help yourselves, you cannot get anything by it. Who by taking care can add to his stature, or make one hair that is white to be black? You may examine and trouble yourselves but you can get nothing by it. Do you think that the Lord will come in mercy a whit the sooner because of the murmuring of your spirits?' Discontent is nonproductive – focusing upon it leads to more discontent because of the inability to change the circumstances or situations that produce the problem in the first place. In the end, the greatest tragedy of discontent is that 'it makes our affliction a great deal worse than otherwise it would be. It in no way removes our afflictions, indeed, while they continue, they are a great deal the worse and heavier.'

RESULTS OF CONTENTMENT

Then what is the benefit of contentment? Why should we even be encouraged and encourage other strugglers to pursue contentment rather than a short-term solution to their problem? Contentment delivers us from an abundance of temptations. 'This is the maxim of the Devil, "he loves to fish in troubled waters;" where he sees the spirits of men and women troubled and vexed, there the Devil comes. Oh, if you would free yourselves from temptations, labor for contentment. It is the peace of God that guards the heart from temptation.' His point is that our discontent increases our vulnerability to temptation. If we are anxious about tomorrow, then we are much more tempted with efforts to try to secure safety for tomorrow as may be happening with an excessive emphasis on saving money (hoarding) or with some obsessive compulsive rituals which are seeking to bring a sense of control and protection over the unknown. Or if we fear that our spouse may leave us, then we are tempted to behaviors today such as suspicious jealousy or emotional abuse. But if contentment is present, the concern may still be present but there is a peace that God can and will lead today and is already aware of tomorrow's problems that we just speculate about. Contentment is not found in obtaining our desires, although God may sometimes grant them to us if they are not harmful. Rather, it is found in finding God in the midst of our unmet desires and in the end discovering that He is all we truly need (Matt. 6:25–33).

Should we pursue contentment in our lives? Should we actively introduce the idea of contentment into our ministry with others? The answer is a definite Yes. Contentment is at the core of the ability to resist temptations, it is the foundation for weathering affliction in a way that results in greater spiritual growth and depth. The emphasis upon trying to solve the surface problems or even deeper problems without recognizing that there is a basic discontent in our hearts, will lead to short-term improvement that will wither under the next period of affliction or difficulty. When working with struggling people, the emphasis must not be solely on helping through the present crisis or struggle (although that help is needed) but as Burroughs continually stresses there is a need to develop a deeper spiritual foundation that will enable them to weather the future storms of life this side of heaven. Without contentment, the temptation to seek it through false means will be present.

Is contentment easy to develop in our lives? Returning to Burroughs initial statement, it is an 'art' and a 'mystery.' So the reply has to be that while it is difficult, it is not so much that the individual has to develop it as to allow God to work this deeper work in their life. Then they will begin to find the contentment that only God can bring as he reorients their entire being to understanding that he is at work and is going to continue to work no matter what their limited perception may be telling them. Contentment is intimately linked with the doctrine of Providence which ties Burroughs work in well with John Flavel's *The Mystery of Providence* (Chapter One). Because there is an element of mystery in the sense of not being reducible to a nice outline of 'tricks' or 'steps' but involving an interactive process with God, contentment cannot be reduced to the pages of this chapter. But as you seek contentment in your lives and in the lives of those you seek to help, there is no better source of help than to consult with Jeremiah Burroughs.

4

WHAT DOES SIN
HAVE TO DO WITH MY PROBLEM?

Conquering Sin Within Us[1]

The year of Shakespeare's death, 1616, was also the year of John Owen's birth, and although Owen was no match for Shakespeare's eloquence, both men did share a remarkable ability to understand human nature. Though Owen put his pen to treatises rather than plays and delivered sermons instead of poems, both men in their distinct ways were able to speak into the complexity of human nature: full of dignity and disease, deception and longing, pride and hope, fear and rest.[2]

This understanding of human nature is exactly why this par-ticular writing of Owen's is important for us today. For it is the understanding of both human nature and how to apply Scripture's truths to that nature that results in the truly effective counselor. 'Owen constantly

---

1 All quotations in this chapter are from John Owen, 'Of The Mortification of Sin in Believers', in *Overcoming Sin and Temptation*, ed. Kelly M. Kapic and Justin Taylor, Crossway Books, 2006, unless otherwise indicated.
2 Kelly M. Kapic, *Communion with God* (Grand Rapids: Baker Book House, 2007), 21.

moves from his received theology to experience, then back to theological reflection. By keeping this reciprocal relationship, with human experience informing theological reflection and theological reflection reforming experience, Owen provides fresh anthropological insights.[3]

On the one hand, Owen demonstrates the absolute necessity of making theology practical in its application to people and their struggles. On the other hand, he demonstrates the tremendous need today for theology to inform human experience, specifically the observations of psychology and the other social sciences on the nature of human beings. Too often, Christians have followed the reverse formula, allowing the observations and experiences of psychological and sociological researchers to determine their theology (in many cases they pay little attention to their theology in the first place!) rather than following Owen's example of a solid theology interacting with experience in a way that truly seeks to find the truths in human experiences and observations but makes them always subservient to Scriptural understandings of human nature. Failure to start from a strong theological understanding of who we are as human beings will result in a dangerous syncretism at best and at the worst may lead to actual denial (even if inadvertent) of biblical truths in the counseling setting.

Owen began his studies at Oxford University but never completed his bachelor of divinity degree there. As he began his pastoral ministry he was actually unsure of his own salvation in Christ until he listened to a country pastor preaching on Matthew 8:26 (he had gone to hear the famous preacher, Edmund Calamy, who was absent and replaced by another). He had begun his ministry as pastor in the small village of Fordham. Because the people were largely ignorant of the Bible, Owen would go from home to home teaching them, eventually utilizing two catechisms that he developed for the young and for adults. By age thirty he was asked to be Pastor at Coggeshall where he would minister to congregations numbering up to two thousand. However, Owen did not remain only a pastor.

3 ibid., 22.

As Oliver Cromwell came into power, he urged Owen to accompany his military expedition to Ireland in 1649 and then later to Scotland as the army's Chaplain. Although reluctant to go, Owen did agree. This step would result in an entirely new trajectory for his life and ministry.

As a result of the expeditions, the House of Commons voted him to be Dean of Christ Church, then considered to be the most prestigious of the Oxford Colleges. Once again he was reluctant because he had not completed his studies at Oxford, and he was only a country preacher and an Army Chaplain. He did not feel he was the man for such a prestigious college of learning, but he did accept the position. While there he also preached on alternate Sundays with Thomas Goodwin at the University Church. Those sermons delivered to undergraduate students were printed later in treatises, including *On the Mortification of Sin in Believers*, the subject of this chapter. An influential voice in the government of England during the time of Cromwell, Owen often preached to Parliament and advised the Lord Protector. Of course, with the return of the monarchy under Charles II, things changed drastically for Owen. Unlike many Puritans, his prestige did protect him from much of the persecution. However he did not abandon his fellow Puritans. He asked his own publisher to take on the task of publishing John Bunyan's *Pilgrim's Progress*, much to the delight of millions of readers since. Charles II once asked Owen why such a man as himself (cultured and educated) would listen to the preaching of John Bunyan, a mere tinker. Owen replied, 'I would gladly exchange my learning for the ability of that tinker to touch men's hearts.'[4] Owen finished the last ten years of his life and ministry as pastor of the church on Leadenhall Street in London.

How should Owen be evaluated? Most consider him to be one of the chief, if not the chief, of the Puritan theologians. And it is typically in this mode that he is viewed, and rightly so. But then why look to a theologian to talk about the practical needs required in

---

4 Robert W. Oliver, 'John Owen (1616-1683) His Life and Times' in *John Owen: The Man and His Theology*, ed. Robert W. Oliver (Phillipsburg, NJ: P&R Publishing, 2002), 35.

biblical counseling? It is because his pastoral concerns are revealed in his writings. Robert W. Oliver concludes

> How should we assess this man of many talents, in turn a country pastor, an army chaplain, head of an Oxford college, vice chancellor before becoming a leader among the persecuted Nonconformists? I suspect that Owen, like so many of his Puritan brothers, saw his real calling to be that of a pastor. That preaching was concerned above all with the glory of God in Christ and the spiritual welfare of his people.[5]

Oliver's evaluation is exactly why his work is important in a book committed to the exercise of biblical counseling. To be effective, counseling ministry must be thoroughly biblical, and be competent in 'diagnosing' the problem of the suffering person and applying Scripture to that problem. In these areas, Owen proves himself highly effective. Kapic even muses that 'I sometimes think of Dr. John Owen as a perceptive physician who delivers both a terrifying diagnosis and the means of a miraculous cure.'[6]

In reading *On the Mortification of Sin in Believers*, I must confess to finding it difficult to read at times, both on an intellectual level – its depth of thought and the usage of grammatical style and words not common today – but also on a spiritual level – it was highly convicting to read in light of my own spiritual life. And yet, I walk away from this magnificent piece of writing, recognizing that Owen is not seeking to condemn us in our sin, but rather desires to point us to the spiritual victory and its accompanying peace and joy, that come from learning how to mortify sin in our lives. In a day when many (Christians and non-Christian) accuse biblical counseling of focusing too much upon sin and thus placing extra burdens upon people, Owen is a breath of fresh air from the past. Focusing upon sin is not ultimately burdensome. It may be initially a burden as we realize how much we have failed and given in to the sinful nature within us, but as Owen demonstrates, focusing

5 ibid., 37

6 Kelly M. Kapic, 'Life in the Midst of Battle: John Owen's Approach to Sin, Temptation, and the Christian Life', in *Overcoming Sin and Temptation*, ed. Kelly M. Kapic and Justin Taylor (Wheaton: Crossway Books, 2006), 24.

upon sin's solution which is Christ, leads us to the victory over sin obtained upon the cross. That victory aids us today through the process of sanctification to find not total victory over sin in this lifetime but certainly relative victory when we engage in the battle to put sin to death.

DEFINING MORTIFICATION

Mortification is a rather strange word for us today so it is helpful to begin with Owen's definition of the process. He begins by referencing Romans 8:13, 'If you through the Spirit do mortify the deeds of the body you shall live.' To mortify means to put to death. The Apostle Paul is instructing believers to put to death the works and desires of the body, referring to the sinful nature. Five specific points are made in this text:

1. A duty prescribed: 'Mortify the deeds of the body.'
2. The persons to whom it is prescribed: 'You' – 'if you mortify.'
3. A promise annexed to that duty: 'You shall live.'
4. The cause or means of the performance of this duty – the Spirit: 'If you through the Spirit.'
5. The conditionality of the whole proposition, wherein duty, means, and promise are contained: 'If you,' etc.

'The "body," here is taken for that corruption and depravity of our natures whereof the body, in a great part, is the seat and instrument, the very members of the body being made servants unto unrighteousness thereby (Rom. 6:19). It is indwelling sin that is intended.' Owen is stressing that the actual physical body is just an instrument, a way in which sin may reveal itself, but the sin itself comes from the heart, the inner person. He later describes Martin Luther before he accepted that we are justified by faith through Christ's death for us. Luther had been characteristic of the 'monkish approach of whipping their bodies' and starving themselves, in other words mistreating the physical body to try to keep sin and sinful desires in check. But the body is simply the way in which the sinful desires of the inner person are able to take action. So if we only focus on the outward displays or behaviors of our sin, then we will fail to put it to death. We must put it to death in our heart.

Owen does distinguish between believers and unbelievers as he notes that the text is clearly speaking to 'you believers, you to whom 'there is no condemnation' (v. 1), you that are 'not in the flesh, but in the Spirit' (v. 9); who are 'made alive by the Spirit of Christ' (vs. 10-11). The pressing of this duty immediately on any other is a notable fruit of that superstition and self-righteousness that the world is full of – the great work and design of devout men ignorant of the gospel (Rom. 10:3–4, John 15:5).' People everywhere seek to be religious and moral by their own means but only believers can truly put sin to death because only believers have the necessary work of the Holy Spirit in their lives. 'All other ways of mortification are vain, all helps leave us helpless; it must be done by the Spirit.' We may attempt to put to death sin by many other ways, as people have always tried to do throughout history, but Paul stresses that it is solely the work of the Spirit, without his power all of our efforts will be worthless (Rom. 9:30–32). 'Mortification from a self-strength, carried on by ways of self-invention, unto the end of self-righteousness, is the soul and substance of all false religion in the world.' Man made attempts will always fail to destroy sin and bring righteousness. Righteousness can only be found by receiving Christ's righteousness as our own through salvation, and then allowing the Holy Spirit to continue his work of destroying the presence of sin in us. Any other approach would be moralism, seeking in our own strength to be 'good', to be moral. But this outer covering of morality will be insufficient to keep the sinful nature in check.

The subject of the inner sinful nature can be confusing for many Christians. Sometimes they ask the question, When we accept Christ into our life as the one who paid for our sin, is not the sinful nature destroyed, gone forever? Why do we have to 'mortify' sin in our lives more than once? Owen explains that to mortify means 'to take away the principle of all his strength, vigor and power, so that he cannot act or exert or put forth any proper acting of his own.' That is, the sinful nature is not destroyed fully until we reach heaven, so its power is still at work in us, and to mortify is to take away the strength of that remaining sin nature to exert its influence upon us. He, therefore, challenges believers, 'do you make it your daily work? Be always at it while you live, be killing sin or it will be killing you. When sin lets us alone we may let sin alone, but sin is never less quiet than when it seems to be most quiet (Rom. 7:23, James 4:5, Gal. 5:17).'

It requires constant warfare to overcome sin in our lives, 'the Spirit and the new nature are given unto us that we may have a principle within us whereby to oppose sin and lust.' As Paul demonstrates in Romans 6–8, Christ does set us free from sin, in the judicial sense bringing forgiveness, no condemnation (Rom. 8:1), but also in the sense that we are no longer slaves to sin (Rom. 6:5–11) so that we no longer must obey it. Further, we can choose to grasp the power of the Holy Spirit to overcome sin in our lives (Rom. 7:24–5; 8:9–11). But it is obvious that the sinful nature remains within us or Paul's discussions in Romans 8 to choose the Spirit and not the flesh would make no sense. So, in the counseling process, sin is a relevant subject because it is always capable of bursting forth in the midst of difficulties.

But as we seek to help people who come for counseling, many today feel that sin is not the problem, their negative feelings about themselves, or the grief they struggle with from a tragedy, or the physical problems of their brain or their body are the problem. They would wonder why they should be concerned about putting to death sin in their lives. And some counselors accuse pastors of spending all their time talking about sin which places a bigger burden on the struggling individual. On the other hand, G. K. Chesterton (early twentieth century), speaking to his critics who said it was 'morbid' to confess your sins, replied that 'the morbid thing is not to confess them. The morbid thing is to conceal your sins and let them eat away at your soul, which is exactly the state of most people in today's highly civilized communities.'[7] Owen would agree with Chesterton, 'where sin, through the neglect of mortification, gets a considerable victory,

---

7 G. K. Chesterton, *Daily News*, January 8, 1908 quoted in Dale Ahlquist, *Common Sense 101: Lessons from G. K. Chesterton* (San Francisco: Ignatius Press, 2006), 200.

it breaks the bones of the soul (Ps. 31:10, 51:8), and makes a man weak, sick, and ready to die (Ps. 38:3–5) so that he cannot look up (Ps. 40:12, Isa. 33:24).'

Events may occur in the believer's life that are not sinful on the person's part but the sinful nature lies in wait to spring forth anytime there is weakness or struggle or even when there is joy. The wise counselor will always remind people that an awareness of the presence of sin and the need to put it to death is part of overcoming any struggle they are experiencing. Otherwise, they risk allowing indwelling sin to enter into their struggle. For example, a tragic death of a loved one may occur. The surviving person may struggle greatly with grief and this is to be expected (Christ himself struggled with grief at the death of Lazarus, John 11:33). But in their grief, the sinful nature lies in wait to try to drive them to despair or to doubting the goodness of God in the mysterious times that we do not understand. Helping them through their grief requires the counselor to remind them of the presence and power of sin that can lead them astray and also encourage them to the daily process of putting sin to death in the specific ways in which they may face current danger. Of course, in many cases, indwelling sin is already involved in the struggle or may be the direct cause of the struggle itself. Mortification of sin is for all believers as a daily discipline, and surely is all the more necessary for those who are in the midst of struggles that require counseling assistance.

Owen repeatedly insists that the struggle with sin is not centered on the body, on our outward behaviors but rather upon what is occurring in our inner person. 'The body is the instrument, or the means, of exercising the sinful desires and may even be involved in the temptation to sin through some weakness or illness, but it is not itself the place from which the sin arises, that is in the inner person, in the sinful nature within us.' So while exercising bodily discipline is commanded by the Apostle Paul (1 Cor. 9:24–7) and is useful, it is not sufficient to put to death the sin within us. Even in the passage in Corinthians he uses bodily exercise to point believers to the more important issue of spiritual exercise and victory. Our enemy is not simply outside us or within our sinfully affected bodies, but ultimately the enemy is within us and there we must be certain the spiritual battle is being fought.

He also stresses over and over that sin must be put to death daily.

> This then, is the first general principle of our ensuing discourse: sin does so remain to act and work in the best of believers, while they live in this world, that the constant daily mortification of it is all their days incumbent on them. He who does not kill sin in his ways takes no steps towards his journey's end. He who finds not opposition from it, and who sets not himself in every particular to its mortification, is at peace with it, not dying to it.

MORTIFICATION IS THE WORK OF THE HOLY SPIRIT IN US

How then do we go about this process? How does putting sin to death relate to the disciplines of the Christian life such as prayer and Bible study that we are clearly commanded to practice daily? The Holy Spirit 'only is sufficient for this work; any ways and means without him are as a thing of naught.' The problem for Owen is that believers often take the disciplines of the Christian life and see them as the actual sources of strength and growth, they think that 'if they fast so much, and pray so much, the work is done. The means will not suffice by themselves, and they will not suffice if exercised in our own strength and wisdom. They must be exercised by the power of the Holy Spirit to the end of allowing God to work in our lives.'

Today, the same error is reflected by those who feel that simply having the outward signs of holiness indicates a conquering of sin. Or some even imitate the Medieval monks by self-mutilation, cutting their bodies, or in other ways seeking to harm themselves in order to try to find relief from their guilt or fear or other troublesome feelings and situations. People have always sought false remedies for trying to overcome sin, but all those remedies leave the person worse than before they were tried. Only in the work of the Holy Spirit in their lives, putting sin to death, will they begin to be able to overcome its terrible effects. As a daily discipline, putting sin to death, works with the other more commonly identified spiritual disciplines. But all disciplines must rely on the power of the Holy Spirit to be effective in our lives.

But Paul is also commanding us as individuals to mortify sin. So what is the role of the individual believer in the process?

> There are three general ways to describe the work of the Spirit in putting sin to death in the lives of believers. First, by bringing the fruits of the Spirit into our lives in opposition to the desires of the flesh (Gal. 5:19–21 with vs. 22–23). Second, by working directly on the roots of sin in our lives, he is called a 'spirit of judgment and… burning' (Isa. 4:4). And thirdly, he brings the cross of Christ into the heart of a sinner by faith, and gives us communion with Christ in his death and fellowship in his sufferings.

The Holy Spirit works 'in us and with us, not against us or without us; so that his assistance is an encouragement as to the facilitating of the work.' In other words, as Paul shares in Philippians 2:12–13 it is both the work of God in us to accomplish his purposes, a work that is impossible without his working in us, but it is also us 'working out our salvation with fear and trembling.' We seek to obey in the process of putting sin to death and as we do so the Holy Spirit assists and makes that work possible. It is not us working alone nor is it the Holy Spirit working alone, not either-or but both-and! In counseling settings, both extremes present themselves. Some overemphasize the role of man by in essence setting God aside while they go out to overcome and remove the identifiable sins in their lives. But in essence they go forth without God. Others overemphasize God's role by identifying sin in their lives and then passively look to God to miraculously remove the sin without any effort on their part. The passage in Philippians stresses that the extremes will leave us vulnerable to ongoing sin, we must seek the both-and in the process of sanctification by trusting in God alone as the source of power but then exercising the new freedom over sin that we have in Christ by acting it out in our daily lives.

Owen stresses again that putting sin to death must be a daily occurrence. 'The life, vigor, and comfort of our spiritual life depend much on our mortification of sin.' We desire to have strength and comfort, and power and peace, in our walk with God. And our struggles can often be related to the absence, or seeming absence, of one of these in our lives. Mortification is not the direct cause of these in our lives as they are a product of our adoption as God's children. Yet 'every unmortified sin will certainly do two things: It will weaken the soul and deprive it of its strength. It will darken the soul and deprive it of its comfort and peace (Ps. 38:3).' It diverts the heart as it 'lays hold on the affections, rendering its [sinful] object beloved and desirable, so expelling the love of the Father (1 John 2:15, 3:17); so that the soul cannot say uprightly and truly to God, "you are my portion," as it has something else that it loves.' It keeps the thoughts focused not upon God but upon trying to fulfill the desires of the sin dwelling in us. 'As sin weakens, so it darkens the soul. It is a cloud, a thick cloud, that spreads itself over the face of the soul, and intercepts all the gems of God's love and favor. It takes away all sense of the privilege of our adoption; and if the soul begins to gather up thoughts of consolation, sin quickly scatters them.' If sin is not put to death, it defines our world, it conforms us to its desires, behaviors and ways of thinking (reversing the process of Romans 12:1–2). You can see this in the person struggling with alcohol or drugs, as the drug becomes their most loved object in the world and it ends up determining their behaviors and even their way of thinking so that others can recognize and say he 'thinks like the alcoholic.' What they are saying is that he no longer thinks like a child of God, seeking to be like Christ. As long as the sin is not mortified, he will follow the direction set by indwelling sin rather than seeking to be more like Christ.

WHAT MORTIFICATION IS NOT

Puritan writers are famous for specifying what something is not, and Owen does not disappoint as he clarifies what actions we take which are not actually putting to death of sin. First, we must understand that 'to mortify a sin is not utterly to kill, root it out, and destroy it, that it should have no more hold at all nor residence in our hearts. It is true this is that which is aimed at; but this is not in this life to be accomplished.' So mortification is not the removal of the sinful nature, nor is it always the complete removal of any given sin. Of course, says Owen, a man sets out to totally destroy sin in his life, so that he will no longer be tempted or led into moral failure. Sometimes we do achieve great success against a specific sin, yet even then 'an utter killing and destruction of it, that it should not be, is not in this life to be expected (Phil. 3:12).'

Many times strugglers want to give up the fight because they find themselves failing over and over and yielding again to the sin they have been struggling with. This would be especially true of areas such as drugs and alcohol, or fear or anger. But the key point for them to remember is that it is not the total conquest of the sin that points to their faithful obedience but their willingness to stay in the battle and keep seeking to put the particular sin to death. So their response after a failure becomes vitally important, do they wake up the next morning and berate themselves for their failure and then say 'why bother, I may as well quit trying and just give in to the sin,' or do they say 'God, I have sinned in the same way again, there is no excuse but I ask your forgiveness for the sin and your help to try to mortify this sin in my life today.' The second response is the biblical one and will enable the person to grow in faith, and probably begin to see at least small growth in their ability to combat their particular sin.

Secondly, Mortification is not the improvement of a quiet nature –

> someone is never so much troubled all his life, perhaps, with anger and passion, nor does he trouble others, as another person is almost every day; and yet the latter has done more to the mortification of the sin than the former. Let not such a person test their mortification by such things as their natural temper. Let them bring themselves to self-denial, unbelief, envy, or some such spiritual sin, and they will have a better view of themselves.

Having a quiet, 'laid back' nature, to use a modern term, does not necessarily indicate that sin is mortified or not present. Although all of us are sinners, it is true that we wrestle with different sins based upon our personalities and life situations. Actually the person with a quiet nature may find themselves sinning in following that very nature. Kelly Kapic catches this notion, 'those who are naturally gentle and pleasant may be surprised to find themselves far down a path that they should have courageously departed from long ago.'[8] Too often believers avoid conflicts, especially confronting another brother in sin, or confronting obvious injustice, by hiding behind expressions of being compassionate and loving when the truly loving process is 'speaking the truth in love' (Eph. 4:15). In these instances, Burroughs would argue they are not truly loving God or their neighbor but confusing contentment with feeling 'laid back' rather than with being truly in the will of God in the situation.

Thirdly, 'a sin is not mortified when it is only diverted.' Here Owen points to Simon Magus (Acts 8:23) who initially responded to his experience with God by leaving his practice of magic, but his covetous and ambitious nature remained and led him back into sin. The problem is that he (and we) will set ourselves against the outwardly obvious sin but not put to death the sin in our hearts, with the result that the sin shows itself in another way in our lives. This occurs commonly in the field of addictions or idolatries when people may give up their addiction or idolatry to something by a force of their will but then simply switch to a 'sociably acceptable' addiction that no one, including themselves identifies as sin, or at least is trivialized as being a 'minor sin.' Or many today display a marked ignorance of the presence and dynamics of sin as they have been influenced by the humanistic belief that we are basically good people so that they accept the lie that they are really a good person who at times does something wrong. Instead, they need to focus on being a sinner who does evil things by their nature but in Christ they can act in righteous ways by depending on his power in the day to day struggles of life. Sin is never trivial because no matter how 'small', it points us back to the unmortified sinful nature within us.

Fourthly, 'Occasional conquests of sin do not amount to a mortifying of it.' These occur when some particularly difficult event has occurred and the person realizes their sinfulness, wakes up to it you might say, so that he cries out to God for deliverance. The person is awakened to the sin and its consequences so that

---

8 Kapic, *Overcoming*, 29–30.

the sin appears to be dead, powerless to further bother him. Owen compares this to a sniper who sneaks up on the enemy camp at night and from a distance shoots the commanding officer. Instantly, the entire camp will be aroused and guards will begin searching for the sniper. But a well trained sniper will hide himself, motionless, until everything quiets down and then move to his next opportunity. So with us, we respond to our committing the sin by rousing our entire being to fight against it, but in thinking it is no longer a threat, we leave ourselves vulnerable to its reappearance when an opportunity of difficulty or struggle may arise that distracts us from our previous alert state. This is why in counseling, we may see a person in a time of great struggle (a divorce, a terminal disease) suddenly struggling with sinful thoughts and responses. The sin had long lain quiet in their heart but now in a time of great struggle, it shows itself again. Sin is adept at hiding within us, allowing us to believe we have conquered it when all we have truly done is recognize its presence and become sorrowful at its activities. Mortification must be a focused and thorough attack upon the sin dwelling within us, and an ongoing discipline in our lives.

PRACTICING MORTIFICATION

Of course, the ultimate question is how do we and those we seek to help actually put sin to death in our lives? It is certainly more than a declaration we make in prayer. 'Mortification consists in a habitual weakening of sin. The first thing in mortification is the weakening of this habit, that it shall not compel as formerly that I shall not be enticed and drawn aside.' Paul speaks of 'crucifying the sinful nature with its passions and desires' (Gal. 5:24). To crucify provides the image of taking away the power of the sinful desires, they will fight hard at first as a man on a cross would fight to live, but eventually they weaken if we keep at the habit of putting them to death. And so, we encourage others not to casually push sin aside, or consider their first overcoming of sin to be the completion of the process, but rather urge the developing of a habitual response to recognizing and reacting to the sin so that it might become more and more weak in their hearts.

The daily discipline, the habit, is important to practice because sin too becomes habitual in our lives. And as we all know from personal experience, 'bad' habits are difficult to break and usually take time as we seek to replace the 'bad' habit with a 'good' habit. Sinfully bad habits must be continually weakened by realizing their presence in our lives, being alert to how they are demonstrating themselves in our thoughts, feelings and action, and daily seeking to weaken them within us.

The corollary to this idea is that 'frequent success against any lustful desire is another part and evidence of mortification.' To habitually respond to the sin when it appears by bringing to bear the teachings of Scripture and the power of the Spirit upon it, will weaken it and evidence that we are truly seeking to put it to death, rather than just temporarily push it aside in order to engage in it at another time. Here Owen notes that learning how sin works is 'practical spiritual wisdom.' As will be seen in more depth in chapter 7 (Precious Remedies Against Satan's Devices), to know and understand how sin works is a vital step in the struggle to overcome it, to 'consider and know where its greatest strength lies – what advantage it uses to make of occasions, opportunities, temptations –what are its pleasures, pretenses, reasoning –what its stratagems, excuses' [is] to set the wisdom of the Spirit against the craft of the old man.'

While sin and the sinful nature will remain with us in this lifetime, the task of mortification is nonetheless always seeking annihilation of the sin currently identified as the enemy, and then seeking to stay alert daily to the temptation to return once again to those sins (1 Pet. 5:8). The important role of a counselor or spiritual mentor is here evidenced. The person who is struggling with tragedy that is not caused by their own direct sin, such as a death or illness, will probably not have the idea of personal sin in their mind. While the counselor's first step will most likely be to provide comfort and encouragement, they must also stay alert to the temptation that this struggle presents for unmortified sin in the person. If the counselor sees specific areas where sin could come into the process, they serve a vital spiritual role by alerting the struggler to the temptation and need to put that sin to death before it can enter into their already difficult time of trial. Owen is stressing that every believer does need to understand their own heart and how sin works in general and specifically in their own life. Otherwise we will always be vulnerable to sin's 'eruptions' and even more so during times of struggle.

For mortification to occur there are conditions that must be present in the persons' life. As previously noted they must be a Christian, for it is the work of the Holy Spirit in the believer's life. Secondly, 'without sincerity and diligence in a universal focus of obedience, there is no mortification.' Israel was often condemned for engaging in fasts or sacrifices but being negligent in serving God in day to day life (Isa. 58, Malachi). So their seeming sincerity in acts of worship was not linked to a spiritual sincerity throughout all of life, no 'universal focus.' Without this complete focus of our lives, the process of putting sin to death will not ultimately succeed. We must be diligent in serving God in particular ways and times but we must also pay attention to our overall spiritual health and obedience. Mortification of sin focuses on a particular sin struggle to be overcome by the believer but in order to be effective in that specific struggle, the believer must also be considering their general spiritual life practices on a daily basis.

> Hatred of sin as sin, and a sense of the love of Christ in the cross, lies at the bottom of all true spiritual mortification. While a man keeps a diligent watch over his heart, its root and foundation – while above all things he keeps his heart, whence are the issues of life and death – lustful desires wither and die in it.

Thirdly, as also previously noted, it must become a part of our daily spiritual habit in order to prevent sin from gaining power from having been ignored. 'If it has lain long corrupting in your heart, if you have suffered it to abide in power, without attempting vigorously the killing of it and the healing of the wounds you have received by it for some long season, your situation is dangerous.' If the sin has been 'hidden' within the heart but allowed to continue with no effort to weaken it, then it will both have the strength to easily come to the surface when the appropriate temptation occurs, and it will easily resist being cast out, as it has firmly taken root in the heart. The other difficulty is that when the thoughts about this sin do arise, the person may seek not to focus on their sinfulness and fighting that sin, but instead will try to focus on what they feel is right about themself and in so doing allow the sin to linger and grow.

INEFFECTIVE WAYS OF MORTIFICATION

Unfortunately, we are capable of deluding ourselves into thinking we are wrestling with sin when we really are not doing so, but are instead trying to reduce the negative effects of the sin, while still trying to hold onto it. 'By applying grace and mercy to an unmortified sin this deceit is carried on (Jude 4). I do not doubt that, through the craft of Satan and their own remaining unbelief, the children of God may themselves sometimes be ensnared with this deceit of sin, or else Paul would never have so cautioned them against it as he does (Rom. 6:1-2).' Paul recognizes that we may minimize sin because we claim God's mercy and forgiveness for it. God does forgive based upon the work of Christ upon the cross, but the heart that chooses sin based on a claim to forgiveness after the action of the sin, is not grasping the true nature of God's work on its behalf. And yet, believers often are attempting to do this very thing. In counseling situations, people may know that what they propose to do is sin, but they feel they must do it (or just simply want to do it) and they are holding out the thought 'that after I commit this sin it will be fine because God will forgive it.' A counselor friend just recently shared about a person who came in to announce they were seeking a divorce. The counselor was sympathetic to their situation but also noted that they did not have a biblically acceptable ground for divorce and that although God will forgive sins we commit, including sinful divorce, we obviously should not commit the sin in the first place. The counselee was extremely angered and stormed out; they were typical of others who are saying, 'I have no choice but to pursue this, and then I'll ask God to forgive me.' This response, although not uncommon, is one more reflection of not seeking to put the sinful nature to death within us, but rather to try to manage it so it is not as bad as it could be! Furthermore, it seeks to take advantage of the grace of God to forgive and forgets the terrible price that Christ had to pay upon the cross to bring us that grace of God.

Owen describes other ways in which we ineffectively try to work with the sin in our lives.

> Frequency of success in sin's seduction is another dangerous symptom. This is that I mean: When the sin spoken of obtains the consent of the will with some delight, though it be not actually outwardly perpetrated, yet it has success. A man may not be able upon outward considerations, to go along with sin to that which James calls the 'finishing' of it (1:14–15), as to the outward acts of sin, when yet the will of sinning may be actually obtained, then has it, I say, success.

Sin in the heart, even if not expressed in outward behavior is still sin. Thus with Christ's teaching in the Sermon on the Mount (Matt. 5) that it is not just the outward behavior but the internal sin that ultimately matters. Resisting the outward expression of sin while allowing the inward success of that sin, is not mortification and will deceive the person into thinking they have achieved success when they have not. In counseling, helping a person find a more effective way of covering up their fear or anxiety may produce seemingly good results in the immediate, but it leaves the person with inward anxiety that has not yet been touched by the struggle to have deeper faith in God, and so their anxiety may now lie hidden but not be truly weakened. This becomes the inherent weakness to behavioral approaches to change. Outward behavioral changes may be helpful in reducing the potential of difficult consequences occurring, but they are not sufficient by themselves for lasting change because they do not address the desires of the heart. It is possible to teach and encourage an anxious person to take part in events that previously they could not engage with, but if there is not also an attempt to help them seek to exercise deeper faith in the Creator God in the midst of their fearful situations, then deeper spiritual change is being ignored. The danger from Owen's perspective is that the person (and counselor) is deceiving themselves into believing they are resisting sin when all they are doing is masking it or pushing it into another way of revealing itself in their life.

Another ineffective way is 'when a man seeks to correct his sin only with arguments from the issue or the punishment due unto it, this is then that sin has taken great possession of the will (James 1:21).' The problem here is that the true motivation for avoiding the sin is 'fear of shame among men or hell from God.' If the fear was not present, they would still commit the sin. What is the true view of sin, something to be avoided in order to appear godly (a people pleaser type of approach) or something that is horribly wrong and offensive before the God who mercifully saved us? While it is common to try to teach people to think about the consequences of their actions before they commit them, this is not equivalent to putting sin to death. Consequence thinking can certainly help us in the battle to resist committing actual sin and is clearly instructed in the wisdom literature, particularly in the opening chapters of Proverbs (chapters 3 and 4 for example). But to realize the consequences is only to resist the outward commission of the sin, not to strike at its core in our inner being.

Furthermore, people often reflect this approach through the commonly observed response of keeping the laws of the state simply because they are afraid of being caught and punished. We have speed limits on our highways and many believers will disobey those limits unless they see a policeman is nearby to catch them and fine them for the crime. But if they feel they cannot be caught they will continue on their way. Or we find how easy it is to sin in 'private' when no other person is watching (of course God is always aware!). These represent the seeming outward righteous response as coming solely from fear of consequences rather than a genuine attempt to attack the actual sinful motive internally. In the speed limit illustration, the inner sin might be that of lawlessness, believing that we can make the laws apart from God and in this specific example apart from his appointed governmental leaders. Fear of consequences as a motive for fighting sin will not put the sin to death. For, if the consequences are not obviously present, then we will feel free to engage in the sin. Instead Owen challenges people to examine their behaviors and their hearts.

> What was the state and condition of your soul before you fell into the entanglements of that sin which now you so complain of? Have you been negligent in duties? Have you lived inordinately to yourself? Is there the guilt of any great sin lying upon you unrepented of? A new sin may be permitted, as well as a new affliction sent, to bring an old sin to remembrance.

EFFECTIVE WAYS OF MORTIFICATION

Ineffective ways of putting sin to death are perhaps easier to recognize than the effective ways, but Owen's goal is to provide genuine help so he begins to describe how we can effectively resist sin. 'Get a clear and abiding sense upon your mind and conscience of the guilt, danger, and evil of that sin within you.' Of the guilt of it. We often try to make our sin trivial or minor in comparison to other sins. 'Is it not a little one?' How often have we followed this line of thinking ourselves, and seen it in helping others. 'Well, I know I should love my family more, but at least I am not out drinking or gambling like others I know.' By comparing to other sins, we trivialize our own, instead of following Owen's direction to feel the true guilt of our sin, potential or actual, so that we will be encouraged to engage in the battle against it. Owen points out that 'Sin seeks in many ways to divert the mind from making a correct appraisal of it (Hosea 4:11).' If we allow this to happen we will never experience the peace and comfort of Romans 8:1 that there is now no longer any condemnation of sin for the believer because of the work of Christ on our behalf. But to experience that peace we must recognize that while ultimate judgment for sin has been accounted for by Christ as our substitute, we are still called to a daily judgment of the continuing sin in our lives. That is, the personal relationship to Christ is based upon Christ's justifying work and his righteousness, not upon our own. Nevertheless, as Christians we are called upon to put to death those destructive sinful ways in us, no matter how trivial the sin may appear. To ignore this responsibility is equivalent to atheism (Owen's term), living as if God does not exist, and therefore I have no moral responsibilities.

Owen continues further by directing you 'should load your conscience with the guilt of sin. Not only consider it has guilt, but load your conscience with the guilt of its actual eruptions and disturbances.' His point here is not to increase our suffering but to increase our awareness of the depth of the sin in our lives. The result will be to drive us deeper in our understanding of what God has done for us in Christ, 'is this the return I make to the Father for his love, to the Son for his blood, to the Holy Spirit for his grace?...Do I account communion with God of so little value that for this vile lust's sake I have scarce left him any room in my heart?' This is not a popular thought in our modern day as people who are struggling through life just want to feel good and experience God's blessing now in ways they can see and feel. But Owen is indicating that if we do not recognize the depth of our sin, no matter how trivial it may appear to us (or to others for that matter), then we are not truly recognizing the incredible suffering of Christ upon the cross to not just bring forgiveness for sin but also free us from the power of that sin (Rom. 6–8). If we minimize our sin, then we choose to trivialize or practically deny the work of God through Christ upon the cross, 'love, mercy, grace, goodness, peace, joy, consolation – I have despised them all, and esteemed them as a thing of naught, that I might instead harbor a lustful desire in my heart.'

If the discussion stopped here, we would all be like those who seem to wallow in their guilt, always bearing the burden of their sinful failures but Owen continues, being thus affected with your sin, 'in the next place get a constant longing, breathing after deliverance from the power of it. Suffer not your heart to be content with your present condition.' God does not intend for us to stay in a guilty state, being overwhelmed by those feelings, rather the guilt should urge us on in the process of confession to find the forgiving grace of God for the acts of sin, and the power of God for putting to death the future sin. But for Owen this should not be a casual process but one in which we are longing for or 'panting' after the grace of God which delivers us from both the guilt and the sin itself (Pss. 38, 42). The glory in guilt is that there is always a solution to the pain of guilt – confession and repentance which will then bring God's forgiveness and remove the burden. We encourage strugglers to avoid both extremes – minimalizing their sin as if it is of no real import or carrying their load of guilt themselves. Instead, putting sin to death involves realizing its full action and import in our lives but then bringing that sin to Christ through confession and repentance to be set free from it.

Owen also encourages the obvious truth that the best time to wrestle with sin is when we first realize its presence before it gains the power of being repeatedly submitted to in our lives. 'Rise mightily against the first actions of your sin, suffer it not to get the least ground. Do not say, "Thus far it shall go, and no farther." If it have allowance for one step, it will take another (James 1:14–15).' Further, he adds that we do not want to be at peace with our sin as we too often are. 'Men certainly speak peace to themselves when their so doing is not attended with the greatest detestation imaginable of that sin in reference whereunto they do speak peace to themselves.' When Job finally realizes his sin (Job 42:6) he 'despises himself' and repents before God. As we come to recognize sin's first terrible actions and truly long for release from it, then we will turn away from our own sense of power to look to Christ for the ability to destroy the sin in us, 'set faith at work on Christ for the killing of your sin.' We are weak and grow weary of fighting with our sin, yet there is always enough strength and ability to overcome given to us by our relationship to Christ (Phil. 4:13).

Which brings Owen at the end back to the work of Christ upon the cross which is essential for anyone to be able to wrestle with and overcome the sin that is destroying their life. 'Mortification of sin is peculiarly from the death of Christ. It is one eminent end of the death of Christ, which shall assuredly be accomplished (1 John 3:8, Titus 2:14). Now this is the powerful work of the Spirit: He convinces of sin (John 16:8–10). He alone can do it.'

CONCLUDING THOUGHTS

In our modern age, most people (and perhaps many of you reading this chapter) find Owen's thoughts to be 'old-fashioned,' part of that supposed historical tradition that emphasizes only sin and our failures in the Christian life. I do hope you will not walk away from this chapter with that type of inaccurate and despairing feeling. On the contrary, Owen talked about recognizing sin and directly and firmly wrestling with it because he cared about people and wanted them to experience the love, blessing, and ultimately peace of God in their lives. But he recognized that from Genesis 3 onwards, people have always had the problem of indwelling sin and that as believers, sin is not destroyed entirely, rather we are freed from its all-controlling power over us. How sad it is then that we so often yield to sin, minimizing in our minds its effects in our lives, redefining it as too often happens in psychologized circles today, or simply trying to convince ourselves it does not matter because we have been justified from our sin through Christ's work on the cross. Owen's intent is not to burden us down with guilt and sin, rather he shows us how to engage in this absolutely necessary battle of putting sin to death daily that we might experience the delivering grace and power of God. Only then will we be able to experience the peace and blessings that Owen indicates all people are desiring.

As you read his discussion, it is quite apparent that Owen knows the hearts of people (himself included!) and so his discussion is truly pastoral and counseling in orientation. Counselors today too often shy away from talking about sin, feeling it just places more of a burden upon the struggler in front of them. But the truth of Scripture is that we live in a fallen, sinful world and so even when our immediate struggle is not due to our personal sin, it is nonetheless caused by sin in the world, and as any observant reader of Scripture knows, trials also tend to reveal our heart and the sins they are still holding onto. Owen recognized this and therefore issued his challenge to mortify sin to believers who are feeling comfortable in their lives (no immediate tragedy or struggle is upon them), to wrestle with their specific sins, not only for the purpose of sanctification today but also for the purpose of being prepared to weather the storms that will come in the future because of this sinful world we live in. Looking at Job chapter 1 makes one realize that Job lived his life in such a way that he sought righteous living, including wrestling with sin every day (1:5) and it was this commitment which prepared him for the horrendous crisis that was soon to come upon him. His initial response was one of faith and belief in God because his was a spiritually prepared life, but even with his preparation the process of wrestling through the tragedies still revealed sin in his own heart that had not been put to death – the sin of believing he could speak about and define God based on his own understandings, rather than upon God's nature and revelation.

Job stands as an excellent example of those who find themselves in a struggle because they live in a sinful world, not because of their own direct sin, but nonetheless through the process of working with the problems, their heart is exposed for further growth. It is no accident that Owen does reference Job as it is apparent that he was very aware of both these scenarios – direct sin to be confronted and a sinful heart to be confronted as it reveals itself in its desires about how to handle the struggles it faces. Counselors would do well to learn this important truth and practice it with those they seek to help, otherwise they may find themselves inadvertently offering the wrong advice suggested by Job's friends. What are often called surface issues in people's lives are important to address as are their perceptions of their struggles, but the deeper work of heart change is the biblical counselor's role and aim in the process. To do less is to fail those we help even if they walk away feeling better. Our culture of therapy too often is satisfied with feeling better without addressing the deeper causes of our initial pain. Counseling too often finds that direction to be easier and thus walks into the deception with the hurting person. Owen challenges us to have a much deeper understanding of how sin is active in our lives this side of heaven and in all situations of life it is a relevant concern. Thus putting it to death is a general daily discipline as well as a distinct work in the midst of events that reveal specific sin.

In *On the Mortification of Sin in Believers* Owen does not directly help us with issues such as anxiety or depression or addictions, but he does much more by pointing us to the heart struggles that both help to form these problems and that surface in the midst of the struggles with these problems. I can only encourage those who seek to help fellow strugglers to follow Owen's advice themselves and offer this direction to others – make the identifying and putting to death of sin a discipline to be practiced in all our lives and ministry activities.

5

NO ONE UNDERSTANDS MY PROBLEMS

Life as a Christian Pilgrimage[1]

John Bunyan was born near Bedford, England in 1628. He was poorly educated, attending school for only a few years. As a child, his moral character was certainly not high but was probably similar to most poor children living around him. He fought as a soldier during the English Civil War (1644–7). He married a poor woman whose father had been a believer and apparently provided her with a dowry consisting of two books – *Plain Man's Pathway to Heaven* and *Practice of Piety*. She would sit and read these two books with John but for a long time he was unimpressed spiritually. Over time numerous influences came together – a sermon on Sabbath-breaking, the sharing of a friend that sent Bunyan to reading a Bible, severe spiritual conflict over whether he had committed the unpardonable sin – these various influences brought him to accept Christ. He was never formally educated as were the other Puritan writers in this book, but

1 All quotations in this chapter are from Bunyan's *Pilgrims Progress*, eleventh edition, published by Fleming H. Revell Company, 1903, unless otherwise indicated.

he learned the Scriptures and received the respect of such Puritan greats as John Owen, who ensured that *Pilgrim's Progress* was made available by recommending it to his own publisher to print. John was not a prosperous man, working as a tinker (a traveling metal worker) and then in the years from 1655 to 1660 he began preaching wherever he could. Because he was not licensed to preach he was arrested and put in the Bedford County Jail (arrested 1658, imprisoned in 1660). For the next twelve years this would be his home (except for a brief period of several weeks). To be released all he would have to do was sign a pledge not to preach without a license. Some others would sign the pledge and then return to preaching, but John stayed true to his convictions that he could not agree to cease preaching if God put that upon his heart, and so he refused to sign. While in jail, Bunyan was industrious as he engaged in the art of making long-tagged thread laces for sale to raise funds for his family outside of jail. He also began writing and in 1676 wrote the first part of *Pilgrim's Progress* although it was not published until 1678. Part two was published in 1685. In 1672 he was released from jail because of Charles II's Declaration of Religious Indulgence. He then became a pastor in Bedford, although he was imprisoned again briefly in 1675 when Charles II withdrew his Declaration. However, Bunyan's popularity resulted in a release after six months and he continued as pastor until his death in 1688.

Pilgrim's Progress immediately resonated with English readers with 11 editions being published between 1678 and 1688. Since then millions of people have read the book all around the world. As an analogy, it functions well as a narrative story describing the entrance into the Christian life and the nature of the journey for a Christian through this world. In choosing this form to write Bunyan was able to grab people's hearts with the idea of an epic narrative while also being able to include direct teaching about strengthening the Christian life and avoiding the temptations and false teachings of his day. Obviously, it took on a timeless value as evidenced by its large readership to this day. As such, it serves here as a valuable resource to ask how this Baptist, itinerant preacher in the Puritan tradition was able to provide biblical counseling through a narrative format. In this chapter, we shall focus only on Part one, the story of Christian traveling to the Celestial City. Part two relates the story of Christian's family eventually following him into the Christian life.

Much of our counseling today tends to focus on helping people achieve insight and then applying cognitive or behavioral solutions to these insights through didactic, teaching methods. While sometimes effective, counselors often find their counselees struggling to deeply apprehend what is being taught to them. This can become especially true in cross-cultural settings where insight and direct teaching are not the common forms of offering help. In *Pilgrim's Progress*, Bunyan seeks to address this problem in his day, not by forsaking teaching but by placing that teaching within the analogy of a journey through life. The journey becomes the framework for sharing his thoughts and also an extremely practical way to help people by allowing them to place themselves alongside Christian, or Faithful, or Hopeful in their day to day struggles to walk down the road. Too often people feel that their struggle is so unique that no one has ever walked through it before. Identifying with the characters in *Pilgrim's Progress* is one way to demonstrate the universality of our struggles. Today, postmodernism emphasizes the concept of narrative as a means to reach people and they do so rightly. Where they typically fail is in their reluctance to make statements of absolute truth from God's Word in those narratives (which Bunyan unashamedly does based upon Scripture) or to move to the opposite extreme of using only narrative and no didactic teaching methods (Bunyan does both although he maintains the narrative format by placing the teaching in dialogue form).[2]

Should a counselor only seek to utilize storytelling, narratives, in counseling? No, but modern day counseling practices have tended to downplay the importance of this method of communicating truth as we seek to help others grow. One way to use narrative is to walk a counselee through a particular narrative in Scripture, such as Joseph's story (Gen. 37–50) or David's story (1 Sam. 16–24) or Mary's

---

2 Tom Steffen in *Reconnecting God's Story to Ministry: Crosscultural Storytelling at Home and Abroad* (La Habra, CA: Center for Organizational and Ministry Development, 1996), 119–127, notes uses of narrative storytelling in the context of missions, which are equally applicable within the realm of counseling methodology.

story (Luke 1–2 and throughout the remainder of his Gospel account). But we could also walk a struggling believer through Bunyan's book to help them truly make this difficult time in their life part of the journey or narrative of their entire spiritual life. Helping them to see others who have struggled and overcome can be encouraging and also helps them see beyond the struggle of today to a wider view of that struggle as being part of a much larger journey. The imagery of Hebrews 12:1–3 does exactly this, providing a view of the Christian life as a marathon race, with ups and downs, struggles and victories along the way.

THE JOURNEY TO THE CROSS

Bunyan begins by describing Christian as a man who is seeking relief because he has heard the message that his city will be destroyed one day because of the evil sin of its inhabitants and so he sets out on a journey away to safety. But his journey is made more difficult by the 'great burden upon his back', which he is unable to remove. For Bunyan, this is a reference to the sin and accompanying guilt that we bear as unbelievers but are unable to remove ourselves because true justice demands a price that we cannot pay. Revisiting the initial point of conversion to Christ with a person can be helpful, not only as a reminder of their salvation but also as a means of helping ascertain how accurately they understood the Christian life at its outset. As Bunyan will show repeatedly throughout his book, there are many such as Ignorance (whose emphasis is on his own knowledge and understanding rather than upon finding God's wisdom) and Worldly Wiseman (whose emphasis is on being moral, not on taking Christ's righteousness) who say they are on the journey towards God's city but they have come in over the wall rather than through the designated gate; they are trying to continue the journey without having actually come by the way of the cross of Christ. So although they may be spiritually oriented, they have not been set free of their burden and are still trying to carry it themselves. With the burden of sin still intact, it would be no wonder that people are depressed, we all should be just as Christian was, 'what shall I do?' The first concern then, would be to walk the person through Christian's initial steps to compare to their own experience. Did he 'run' from his sin, his lifestyle, to pursue Christ as Christian did? Or did he try to just slide into the church without any deep commitment to Christ, as illustrated in Pliable who starts out but at the first sign of difficulty decides to go back to what appears to be an easier life which in reality is a delusion? If there was no commitment then, now is the time to challenge him to that commitment to Christ. And if he does seem to have genuinely come to know Christ, then it is still beneficial as a counselor to reinforce that conversion as the foundation for how to wrestle with his current struggles.

Christian's first experience is to suddenly fall into the 'slough of Despond' and find his search immediately being challenged as Pliable asks 'Is this the happiness you have told me of all this while, if we expect such ill speed at our first setting out, what may we expect between this and our journey's end?' Pliable starts by believing that seeking God will be all ease and good feelings, instead of recognizing that in this still sinful world, following God will entail struggles and difficulties, but in persevering through we will find God's presence was there with us even when we could not see it. Faced with difficulties, Pliable chose to turn back. Christian, although discouraged, continued to persevere and ultimately found freedom through the efforts of Help, who informs him that 'as the sinner is awakened about his lost condition, there arise in his soul many fears and doubts, and discouraging apprehensions, which all of them get together and settle in this place (the slough of Despond).' God's offer of Help is not always obvious when we first seek it but He does respond to those who seek him (Isa. 55, Jonah 3:6–10, Rom. 10:8–13) and provides help in every struggle to those who have given their lives to him (1 Cor. 10:13). But to find Help we first experience struggle, otherwise we have no sense of our need of Help. A struggler's current problems represent an opportunity to open his eyes to try to see a new reality around him, one in which he can begin to sense and see God's presence in ways that may appear mysterious or confusing to him at first glance but nonetheless demonstrate God's active involvement in his daily life.

As he proceeds, Christian still feels the burden of the guilt of sin and desperately looks for a way to remove the burden. Worldly Wiseman initially succeeds in steering him off to what seems to be a way to quickly remove the burden, but Christian is found in time and sent back on the right course by Evangelist. Our sinful hearts consistently strive to remove guilt and the pain of living in a sinful world because we do not like how it feels! We are drawn to all sorts of false ways to remove that pain which may appear to work temporarily but in the end fail us because only Christ can bring that freedom. In our struggles, we will be tempted to try different ways of removing the inner pain we feel such as alcohol or drugs, running away by rashly quitting jobs or ending marriages, finding ways to further numb ourselves (we have myriad different ways of doing this), but just as Christian discovers, it is only Christ who can lift the initial burden of guilt from upon us, and even as believers it still remains only the Cross of Christ that can bring us freedom. Our self determined methods will always fail in the long-run and further wrap us up in addictive styles of pursuing them for relief, having them fail after a time, forcing us back to the addictive activity again, and continuing to reinforce the destructive cycle.

This discussion continues as Christian speaks with Interpreter who explains how Patience waits upon God to bring relief while Passion seeks to 'have all now, this year, that is to say, in this world; so are the men of this world; they must have all their good things now; they cannot stay till next year, that is, until the next world, for their portion of good.' They focus on eating, drinking and being merry instead of enduring struggle and suffering as representative of the life of Christ, but also as recognizing that it is an important part of the journey through this sinful world. The journey has a direction, for Christian it is the Celestial City which represents that final reaching of heaven by the believer, where there will be no more sorrow, pain, crying (Rev. 21:4). It is interesting to note how Evangelist and Interpreter speak to Christian. They are firm and direct, almost seeming uncaring at moments. But Bunyan recognizes that in helping the struggler we must be firm in bringing them truth. For some, this could be a crucial moment in their life, because they may feel that

God has failed them (by not bringing a good marriage or a good job) and they may be ready to step away from the church and spiritual growth. That would be a decision of terrible consequence. It takes the firmness of the truth at times to call people away from all these seemingly easy responses to problems to instead seek to continue with God through the dark and difficult times. Is Bunyan then only concerned with presenting truth with no love? He writes that after speaking firmly Evangelist 'kissed him, gave him one smile, and bid him God-speed.' Evangelist was caring but understood that caring involves firm communication of the truth and confronting. Yet at the same time, he was 'speaking the truth in love' (Eph. 4:15) and was seeking to encourage a tired struggler to continue on in the journey of the spiritual life. A smile, even a sense of humor, can make hard truths much easier to apprehend!

Of course, in Bunyan's story Christian is not yet a believer as he has not come to the cross of Christ. We can use these opening portions of the story to help strugglers examine their own faith experience with Christ, and also point out that these truths experienced by Christian before coming to Christ still remain true as we begin the Christian life also. 'So, I saw in my dream, that just as Christian came up with the cross his burden loosed from off his shoulders, and fell from off his back, and began to tumble, and so continued to do till it came to the mouth of the sepulcher, where it fell in, and I saw it no more.' 'It was very surprising to him that the sight of the cross should thus ease him of his burden.' The paradox of the cross is that an instrument of torture and cruel death becomes the place where we experience the freedom that comes from our guilt being taken by Christ upon that cross, so that as we believe we are truly pronounced without sin any longer, 'there is now no condemnation for those who are in Christ Jesus' (Rom. 8:1). Perhaps for some we seek to help, they never truly experienced Christ's freedom, they came over the wall in their own way rather than following the path to the cross and then beyond it. Or perhaps, in the midst of their problems, they simply need to be encouraged to return back to the cross to recognize what God has already done for them. Many times I have heard believers in counseling settings say 'if only God would do something to show me he cares, then I could move forward through this depression.' At that moment it is always proper to remind them that God already did something – the Cross of Christ says everything that needs to be said about the mercy and compassion of God for us. God does continue to work today, but in those times when we can not see him at work, the cross continues to stand as the supreme example of his mercy, love, and compassion being brought to those who believe, at the price of the horrible death of Christ upon that cross.

THE JOURNEY IN CHRIST IS JOYFUL AND DIFFICULT

Christian's response to the removing of the burden is to head quickly down the road, leaping and singing. Coming to know Christ and experiencing his forgiveness of our sin usually does bring a moment of joy for all of us. But then we find ourselves still in this sinful world and we must be careful to recognize the realities of the sinful world – it can be fearful, depressing, overwhelming – while also trying to remember that the rejoicing we felt at the cross is still true, just more difficult to experience in the trials of life. And this is exactly because our life is a spiritual journey. We tend to look at it through the immediate moment of struggle rather than see it as that journey that Christ began and also finished (Heb. 12:2–3). Just as Christ finished it, we can too if we stay focused upon him as the finishing line of the race, as the end of the journey. Christian is almost immediately confronted with three men: Sloth, Simple, and Presumption, all of whom quickly grew tired and went to sleep rather than continuing the journey. Where is the struggler's spiritual life at now – did they truly come to Christ? Perhaps so, but did they then continue the process of spiritual growth or did they stop to rest upon their initial experience? This is the way of these three men – they went into neutral in their spiritual lives, failing to see the danger that brings. To stop growing is to leave ourselves all the more susceptible when difficult times do come because we have not found the strength to trust in and discern God's will when we cannot see clearly. We must encourage them that the goal is not simply to feel better in their current struggle but more importantly to strive towards spiritual growth through the current struggle, to keep on moving down the road with Christian.

Once upon the road, Christian is continually reminded of the blessing that it is to have come into this life journey through the cross. Others such as Formality and Hypocrisy ask 'If we get into the way, what is the matter which way we get in?' to which Christian replies, 'I walk by the rule of my Master: you walk by the rude working of your fancies. You are counted thieves already by the Lord of the way; therefore I doubt you will not be found true men at the end of the way. You come in by yourselves without his direction, and shall go out by yourselves without his mercy.' The journey is about the starting place, apart from Christ there is no journey that will ultimately be successful and so it is a blessing to know we are on the correct journey through life. This is one way to comfort strugglers in their belief in Christ. But then they must take that blessing as an encouragement to continue on this right journey and recognize it is a journey, they can not just stop at the foot of the Cross and stay there (much as the disciples wanted to do on the Mount of Transfiguration, Luke 9:28–36) because life is a journey through this life to the glories of our ultimate life in heaven. And that journey will not always stay easy as Christian next finds himself at the foot of the hill Difficulty.

> There were also in the same place two other ways, besides that which came straight from the gate; one turned to the left hand, and the other to the right, at the bottom of the Hill; but the narrow way lay right up the hill, and the name of the going up the side of the hill is called Difficulty.

> I looked then after Christian, to see him go up the hill, where I perceived he fell from running to going, and from going to clambering upon his hands and his knees, because of the steepness of the place. Now about the mid-way to the top of the hill was a pleasant arbor, made by the Lord of the hill for the refreshing of weary travelers.

Christian takes the way of difficulty in the journey and in extremely realistic fashion Bunyan notes he is reduced to crawling along, yet he keeps going. Then he finds a place to rest and be strengthened by

God. We often face that moment when we are saying, I can not go on, I do not have the strength. The truth is not that we have to go sprinting up this Hill Difficulty, or even be hiking along at a great pace, but we need to keep going even if it means crawling up. As a hiker I enjoy hiking in mountains at times. But also being someone who is not generally in top aerobic condition, I can remember many a trail where the footsteps cover less and less space, and the controlled breathing has long since lapsed into gasps for air because the trail is steep or the altitude is high. I sometimes want to stop but encourage myself to just keep going, even if slowly. This is Bunyan's picture with Christian, keep going – you will find the strength and refreshing of God along the way, but spiritually overcoming does not mean we waltz our way through difficulties, it means we are able to come through because of God's mercy, although it may be with great fatigue!

After the conquest of the Hill one would think Christian would have an easy time of things but as he moves into a wonderful land, Beautiful, he is first confronted by two menacing lions. He has already been encouraged by Watchful that the lions are chained but their chains are hard to see so he must trust and move past them. Christian has seen that Mistrust turned back because of fear of the lions. 'Then I saw that he went on, trembling for fear of the lions; but taking good heed to the directions of the Porter, he heard them roar, but they did him no harm.' This sinful world presents many dangers and they are truly frightening to us at times. Struggling people may be facing those fears as they look at a life and a world that to them seems to be falling apart and can only become worse. It is at these times when we cannot see distinctly that we must exercise faith. Faith is not based on what we can see but is the 'being sure of what we hope for and certain of what we do not see' (Heb. 11:1). Christian has the word of promise that God will be with him but he also encounters the lions of the enemy (see 1 Pet. 5:8). We should be aware and careful but continue based upon God's view of reality not our own. For many, depressive feelings begin to skew how they see the world around them, there is a tendency for them to begin to catastrophize, to see every event in its worst possible explanation; and to begin to see themselves perhaps as failures in all things or as someone who has been abandoned by everyone. Seeking to accurately see ourselves and our world based upon God's viewpoint is essential to prevent the downward cycle we fear from becoming the truth, not because it had to happen but because our distorted view of reality resulted in us making decisions and responses that bring that distorted view of reality to become our new reality. Recognizing it is a fearful world with enemies, physical and spiritual, and that we must take care is a biblical understanding. But we must always strive to see those fears from the perspective of God who will always be with us in the fear (Isa. 43:1–7, Ps. 23) and will protect us.

But a struggler might ask, what does God's protection look like? Many take God's protection to always appear as it did for Christian with the lions, as we move by we see them to be chained, to be held back from truly hurting us. Not too much later in the story, Christian will experience a different type of protection as he and his friend, Faithful, find themselves imprisoned in the city of Vanity Fair because of their Christian faith. They are tortured and Faithful is protected not by continuing life but in his death as he is taken directly to the end of the life journey to experience blessing in God's presence. Christian is protected not by preventing of the torture but by God's strength in the torture and then eventual release to continue his journey. Too often we interpret God's protection and provision only in a miraculous deliverance understanding instead of seeing it in its deeper, more eternal perspective. This is an important truth to understand lest we look to God for deliverance and then become further depressed because God does not respond in the way we expect.

While resting at the Lodge, Christian engages in long spiritual discussion with the sisters, Prudence, Charity, and Piety. During the discussion, Prudence asks him if he is still carrying with him 'some of the things' that were in his life before the cross. 'Yes, but greatly against my will; especially my inward and carnal cogitations, with which all my countrymen, as well as myself, were delighted. But, now, all those things are my grief; and might I but choose mine own things, I would choose never to think of those things more.' Coming to Christ means forgiveness of sin, freedom from the power of sin, and the coming of the Holy Spirit to dwell in our lives. But the conversion experience does not automatically root out all our wrong thinking and desires. That is why an ongoing commitment is vital for continued growth, along with recognizing that God uses struggles in our lives to continue to move us away from our remaining wrong thinking and desires. Through struggles, our inner heart is revealed and even if the struggle itself is not caused by our direct sin, we still begin to see into the sinful heart that remains, under the pressure of the struggle.

It may not be direct failures that have brought us to the point of despair (then again it may be too!) but even if that is the case, God through the suffering, is giving us a glimpse into our hearts to see where our sinful nature is still at work and urging us to pursue unbiblical responses. Not all our problems are a result of our own sin, but when we are sinned against, it is vital to recognize that our response may reflect our own sinful hearts. Recognizing this does not bring automatic victory, the spiritual life is a journey of growth, not a 100 yard sprint that is run quickly and is over. Lack of awareness prevents spiritual growth because as so many of the other characters in the book demonstrate, being ignorant of your own sinful tendencies makes it impossible to bring them before God to wrestle with and seek to overcome. In that sense, the depression a person feels can become a blessing as it helps them to take a few more steps along the journey to first understand the sinful patterns carried over from their pre-Christian life and then to encourage them to growth in those areas.

As Christian prepares to leave the lodge, they insist he go away with armor, shield, and sword. In an obvious allusion to Ephesians 6:10–18, Bunyan alerts his readers to the necessity of going forth in the journey with all the 'armor' that God has provided for us. Once again, Christian alerts us to the fact that this life is often a war spiritually, not just with our own sinful nature, but with the world and the devil and his demons. If we go forth unarmed then we presume upon God's promises of protection. If we go forth fashioning our own armor, in our own strength, then we will fail when the enemy strikes as he quickly does with Christian. Apollyon appears and first tries to attack Christian's faith with arguments and planting of doubt. He points to Christian's instances of having 'been unfaithful' to God, and asks how he can think he can continue to serve God now? Christian admits 'all this is true' but then notes how Apollyon brings only part of the truth because he does not mention the forgiveness and mercy that God has promised and extended to those who believe in him (1 John 1:9). Finding that he cannot twist Christian away with half-truths he attacks him physically. It is only the armor of God that allows Christian to fight successfully in this the 'dreadfullest fight that ever I saw.' Even then Christian comes out of the fight wounded.

As we seek to apply this part of the story to our lives, we can think of the struggle of depression, the person is involved in a fight as the depression seeks to pull them down and send them into utter hopelessness and despair. Wrong thoughts are rolling about in their mind – this Christian life does not work, I am too sinful for God's mercy to work any longer, another wife would make me happy – and all these thoughts need to be confronted gently but firmly with truth from God's Word. But they also are simply involved in a terrible fight not to be overcome and once again they must seek to fight with God's armor – truth, prayer, dependence – and not seek to fight in their own armor. Moralism fights with armor made from its own wisdom, the Christian must fight with armor based on God's wisdom and so a review of Ephesians 6:10–18 may be helpful, followed by a specific application of how that armor would be worn and exercised in their life at this moment of struggle.

One would immediately think that on the other side of the great victory with Apollyon, that Christian would be off running and sailing along once again. Instead he finds himself in the 'Valley of the Shadow of Death; and Christian must needs go through it, because the way to the Celestial City lay through the midst of it. Now this valley is a very solitary place; the prophet Jeremiah thus describes it; a wilderness, a land of deserts and of pits, a land of drought, and of the Shadow of Death, a land that no man, but Christian, passes through, and where no man dwelled. Now here Christian was worse put to it than in his fight with Apollyon.' Christian experiences what in the Middle Ages was referred to as the 'dark night of the soul.' It refers to those times when all seems dark, we can not see ahead, we certainly can not see God. What do we do? Many want to stop or simply escape back out of the darkness. But the way through the dark night of the soul is to clutch onto what we do know about God and his work in our lives and just keep moving forward one step at a time. Will it be pleasant – No; will it become easier – probably not. But the 'dark night of the soul' is not forever, although it may well feel that way to us! It is a time to just keep 'running the race' or 'crawling the race' and not let the darkness completely overwhelm.

This is a common theme in works of literature (whether by Christians or not) as they detail those who keep going on even when everything appears hopeless, rather than give up. I enjoy reading in the literature of early Arctic and Antarctic exploration and it is full of stories of men who should not have survived but kept pushing on even when they thought survival was impossible – men such as Earnest Shackleton, Douglas Mawson, and a host of others. Most of them did survive (though not all) but the stories of those who felt the despair and impossibility and gave up are also told. I have always been impressed that Douglas Mawson survived even after both of his companions were killed, he was suffering from vitamin A poisoning (not understood at that historical time period), his food was lost in a crevice and he found himself in constant blizzards weeks away from any help, but he kept going for another hundred miles, while Robert Falcon Scott (second to reach the South Pole) in terrible conditions seemed to just give up and die quietly in his tent instead of continuing to try against the odds to fight his way to the next food depot twelve miles away. Although neither of these men's stories are based on their spiritual life with God, they show the understanding in human literature of the dilemma of the 'dark night' – do you keep pressing on or do you give up through suicide or just sitting motionless to die? The stories that grab us most are of those who keep pressing on despite the impossibility of the task. Christian persevered and found his way through the Valley. Struggling people need encouragement to persevere in doing what is biblically right even though it may not seem to yield results and even though their efforts at prayer may seem fruitless – God is there in the dark, it is us that struggle to perceive him.

It is also important to help distinguish between what may be sin in their life (either causative of the current struggles or in response to the current struggles) as versus what is temptation. As Christian struggled through the darkness, we are told that 'one of the wicked ones got behind him, and stepped up softly to him, and whisperingly suggested many grievous blasphemies to him which he truly thought had proceeded from his own mind.' In the midst of depression for example, there will certainly be increased temptations, as they always become stronger when we are weaker. Too often, the fact of the temptation and the ugliness of the temptations felt, leads people further into despair. They ask themselves how a Christian could think such thoughts or desire to do such things? And so, they take temptation not acted upon and label it as sin. Temptation is not sin, yielding to temptation is. Christian was able to see this and recognize that although he disliked the thoughts he was having, they were not a true reflection of his heart and he was refusing to act upon them. So they become simply temptation, serious and strong temptation, but still not sin committed by him. I have seen people in counseling settings burdening themselves with sin that really is not sin but is instead temptation. Aiding them to understand the difference will help them become stronger in the face of the temptations. As he moves on, Christian does hear another voice saying, 'I will fear no ill, for you (God) are with me.' So Christian perceived that God was with him, 'and why not thought he, with me? Though by reason of the impediment that attends this place, I cannot perceive it.' He embraces walking not by sight but by faith. He cannot see God but holds onto the knowledge that God is present in the darkness that his own eyes cannot penetrate. Note that in this darkness it was the voice of another believer that he heard and which helped him to hold onto God. The counselor may well be that other voice in the darkness, encouraging and bringing the truth back to strugglers who are experiencing the darkness. On a final note of reality, Bunyan notes how Christian passed through and then looked back 'by the light of the day' and was able to see accurately what he had just passed through. God will bring those moments when the light appears or the curtain is drawn back and we glimpse accurately what we have gone through but he does not necessarily do so while we are going through the darkness.

OTHER BELIEVERS WALK WITH US

At this point in the counseling journey, the person we are seeking to help may be agreeing with us but feeling very tired, even if they have begun to be able to look back through the light of a new day. It is too early for them to be abandoned by the counselor. They still require the fellowship and strengthening that comes from talking with another believer as they continue to try to move forward. This could be the counselor or another mature believer who steps alongside to help them continue to move forward through the struggles that hopefully are beginning to look different to them now, but are nonetheless still present. Bunyan captures this understanding by having Christian meet up with Faithful and as they continue on together they have long discussions of their spiritual journeys and times of seeking to understand God's Word better. It is even interesting to see how at one moment Faithful is leading Christian into truth, and at the next moment it is Christian leading Faithful into the truth. This serves as an illustration that all of us are truly fellow strugglers along this journey of the Christian life. In the role of counselor, a person is probably approaching me because of some level of expertise and gifting in helping others. That is hopefully correct, but if I as a counselor lose sight of the common journey (common in that we all experience it, although unique in that we do not all experience it exactly the same way in terms of the details and our responses) that we are both engaged in, then I begin to make my help more distant for them. Entering in as a fellow struggler allows me to share my life journey just as Christian and Faithful do with each other, and be able to speak firmly when needed as to the truth I have learned that they may not have learned yet, while at the same time hearing them speak into my life.

As they continue the journey, the two find themselves in Vanity Fair. There is much to distract and lure away in this city which offers all the world's pleasures as something to be experienced without giving any thought to whether they are godly desires or not. To their great credit, Faithful and Christian remain true to their faith and are not tempted away by all the inducements. However, to their surprise they suddenly find themselves being accused of crime because they are not acknowledging the false truths of the merchants of the town. The merchants become angry and beat them and they find themselves arrested for being the cause. Doing the right thing biblically does not always bring good immediate results. Joseph experienced this in Genesis 39 as he resisted temptation and then was 'framed' with a crime he had refused to commit and punished for it. As we seek to take correct biblical responses we have to understand that this may not make all the problems go away. If we refuse to honor an unethical response from a supervisor at work, we may find ourselves being ostracized or even fired rather than honored for taking a bold, just response. Because we are still in a fallen world, true, absolute justice does not yet exist. Christ will bring that justice on his return and setting up of the new heavens and new earth, but for now good responses are sometimes met with bad results. This becomes yet another area where our trust and faith in God is tested. Will we believe he is truly the Judge who will bring justice in his time and way? Or will we say this Christianity thing does not work, so I will just leave it and do whatever I have to do to keep from experiencing bad results? If Christian and Faithful had denied their faith, they would have been released unharmed, but they refused to do so. So too must we when faced with situations where doing the right thing biblically is greeted with negative results instead of positive. Why is this truth important? It is because we will have to make choices about how to respond in the situations we face and after grasping that God is with us, it becomes quite easy to then assume that means that as I take all these right steps, everything will turn out wonderfully. Once again, we end up focusing on everything working out in this life, instead of seeing that God's focus is ultimately on the end of our journey, which he plainly sees but we do not. People will need to be challenged to love their spouses even if that does not seem to bring a positive result in their marriage. They should do the correct biblical things because they are right, not because they will bring a desired result.

As Christian continues his journey after Vanity Fair, he finds himself in conversation with By-ends who notes 'that I had always the luck to jump in my judgment with the present way of the times, whatever it was, and my chance was to get thereby.' In other words, By-ends follows the current fads of society and culture without asking whether they are truly biblical or even an advance upon previous practices. Strugglers will find themselves beset with advice and sorting through it can be difficult at the best of times, let alone when you are already depressed and having trouble concentrating and thinking through issues deeply. A good counselor must always be seeking to guide people through the fads of the day to the lasting biblical solutions that are available. Looking today at the field of psychology and psychiatry we can certainly see some accurate and relevant observations that are being made which may help us as we seek to understand the specific struggles of others. And some of the suggested solutions may be consistent with biblical understandings, either because a particular researcher has a strong biblical foundation or simply because of the presence of God's common grace which allows even those who deny him to discover his truth at times. But any fair observer will also note the up and down, back and forth nature of psychology or psychiatry (as in other fields as well) in which some current theory or two comes to the forefront and is the 'answer' to the struggling person's problems. Not every fad is incorrect, obviously, but the danger of fads is the fact that culturally they sound and feel correct because so many 'experts' are propounding them. Mr. By-ends reveals that way of thinking, see where the wind blows and go with that. Bunyan is very representative of the Puritan writers here as he cautions against just simply accepting the latest 'fad' way of describing a problem and its solution to instead return to the eternal Word of God for a deeper understanding of how to apply it in the context of the modern day problem we are seeing. We must see people's problems in a modern day perspective because that is where both they and I as their counselor are located, yet we must also take care not to ignore history and particularly this ancient book we know as the Bible. At times a biblical understanding agrees with current thought but at many other times we 'must go against wind and tide; the which, I perceive, is against your opinion.' Fads have a habit of cycling back and forth throughout history and will eventually fade if they are not based on God's truth, but the struggling person will grasp hold of a fad easily because it promises a quick and easy solution to their problem! We must guide them back to more biblical applications.

Mr. By-ends continues by saying, 'I shall never desert my old principles, since they are harmless and profitable.' In their interchange, Christian would probably be seen today as intolerant and opinionated when in reality he is trying to point out that wrong principles do have consequences, false 'truth' is never harmless. The same is clearly true in the struggle today to provide counseling that is biblically based. Yes, we should try to stay loving in our discussions, and seek to honor other believers who disagree, but at the same time we must believe that truth matters. Too many believers today believe as do Mr. By-ends, why bother with all these discussions about a proper biblical understanding of depression or how to develop a biblical understanding of body–heart relationship so we can decide what to do with anti-depressant medications? Why not just go with the current flow and not question it, especially if it seems to be helping the person? It is accurate that people can be temporarily helped at times by approaches and theories that are not biblically based, but do we really believe that in the end those approaches will help them long-term if they are not true? The answer is they will eventually fail the person if they are not based on biblical truth (and I have seen this occur many times). So, there genuinely is a battle for biblical truth in understanding who people are, how they struggle, and how we should help the person who sits with us looking for direction. We must remember that our goal is not just to help them now (as the fads sometimes do) but to help them in the context of a long journey. If a person has already bought into the current fads of the day which may not be thoroughly true, then it would be a disservice not to engage them in that discussion. It can and should still be done gently, but firmly for as Christian recognized, those fads are not harmless, they lead us into future error and certainly provide a shaky foundation for our growth in the Christian life. Throughout *Pilgrim's Progress* those who do not keep wrestling with finding God's truth eventually end up straying off the correct path into immense dangers.

Similarly, Hopeful and Christian soon engage in conversation with a cast of characters who try to lead them off after wealth and prosperity. Wealth and prosperity are not necessarily wrong as God may bless in those ways, but it certainly should not be the pursuit of our journey. It is interesting to hear Demas, trying to lure Christian aside to check out the silver mine. Christian asks, 'Is not the place dangerous? Has it not hindered many in their pilgrimage?' 'Not very dangerous, except to those that are careless; but withal, he blushed as he spoke.' Of course, it is dangerous because it can too quickly become the 'addiction' that allows us to temporarily escape our struggle or our pain but in the end entraps us even more. As they turn away, Hopeful comments, 'I will warrant you, when By-ends comes up, if he has the same invitation as we, he will turn in there to see.' Christian: 'No doubt thereof, for his principles lead him that way, and hundred to one but he dies there.' Any given choice at any particular moment by Mr. By-ends may be harmless but the underlying foundation of his thinking leaves him vulnerable to temptation to follow sins that will bring deep and lasting destruction and bondage. That struggle continues today. Even as people begin to try to understand their situation in the light of God more accurately, and seek to ask consistently what is it that God would have them do today, they will probably still feel depressed (at least for a time). If their pursuit is based upon the principle that they may have some error in their thinking or may be following some fads but they are really not harmful at present, they leave themselves open to these much more destructive temptations as illustrated by Demas.

DISCIPLINE IN THE JOURNEY

As the journey continues they come to a river, the River of Life, and find themselves in a time of enjoying the water, the scenery, a rest.

As with the resting place on the Hill of Difficulty, God does provide periods of time in our earthly lives when we are deeply experiencing his peace and joy. That they are not always present does not mean they will not occur. Sometimes when helping people, it is useful to try to ask them to reflect back upon their original salvation experience and other periods when they may have really sensed and felt God's presence at work in their life. These can be memorials to help them now during this period when they do not feel that joy or peace or rest. The journey through life has both the times of trials and the times of refreshment. Remembering the times of rest during the trials is crucial to combating our mind's tendency to base everything on what it is currently experiencing and then project that into tomorrow and the day after so there is no hope. As a counselor, I can not predict when that time of refreshing will come other than in eternity, but I can say it will come for those who continue the journey and do not stop where they are. Even as a person begins to understand the causes for their depression and the steps they need to take, they will need the encouragement of others because understanding and beginning down the correct path does not magically transport you to the River of Life. Often we have to be encouraged to proceed based on faith in God's nature and his previous works in Scripture, Church history, and our own life. Bunyan captures this further as he notes throughout the book how at times Christian will catch sight of his goal – the Celestial City – but then at other times he can no longer see it. Our lives are that way as well, the overcomer is the one who continues on when they cannot see the city, but the encouragers can stand alongside not only to help them up a 'steep slope' but to remind them that their view of the Celestial City was true and they will see it again.

Christian makes the next mistake as he leads Hopeful through a field that looks like the way to go but turns out to be wrong and they find themselves fighting through a flood. They are wise enough to turn back to return to the proper path 'but by this time the waters were greatly risen, by reason of which the way of going back was very dangerous. (Then I thought that it is easier going out of the way when we are in, than going in when we are out.).' When it is our own sin leading us out into difficulty, it is never easy to turn around and come back. In one sense it is easy, repent – turn away from our sin – and confess it to God (and to others if they have been sinned against). But both those steps, asking forgiveness and repentance, are usually difficult for us to take. And the steps of repentance may be slow. If someone has repeatedly failed in their marriage, even asking for forgiveness and beginning to love your spouse more biblically will not necessarily result in immediate positive responses on their part. They may mistrust what is being done even to the point of denying it altogether. The way back through sin can be very difficult but it is always worth it because the way into sin will eventually end in total destruction. For Christian and Hopeful it proves an extremely difficult journey as they fight through the flood only to be captured on the property of the Giant Despair who locks them up and counsels them that they would be better to kill themselves as that will be easier upon them than his torture. Things worsen to the point that 'Christian again seemed to be for doing it; but Hopeful made his second reply.' Hopeful reminds Christian of where they have come from and how they have done so and counsels that they 'bear up with patience as well as we can.' Can a Christian find himself at the point of despair so deep that he considers taking his own life? Yes he can, and that does not indicate he is an unbeliever. Bunyan recognizes the depths we can plunge to and wisely has Christian wrestle with the thought of suicide as the only option. It is a temptation that any believer can feel when they are deeply burdened. Should they respond – of course not! Hopeful's reply stands throughout time as the encouragement to take a deeper look at the real picture of what is happening and then wait patiently upon God for his deliverance. The counselor stands in the place of Hopeful to encourage others to not feel ashamed for their thoughts of taking their own life, but to also encourage them to move away from those thoughts by rehearsing once again who God was, is, and will be in their life, and then urging them to the difficult patience needed in the time of severe trial and testing.

Later they return to this theme as Christian shares about Little-Faith who was robbed of his money and possessions, all but the scroll given to him as his admittance to the Celestial City.

> It might have been great comfort to him, had he used it as he should;
> but they that told me the story said that he made but little use of it all
> the rest of the way, and that because of the dismay that he had in the
> taking away of his money. Indeed he forgot it a great part of the rest
> of his journey; and besides, when at any time it came into his mind,
> and he began to be comforted therewith, then would fresh thoughts
> of his loss come again upon him, and those thoughts would swallow
> up all.

Little-faith loses sight of what God has provided for him because he focuses on what he has lost (or not gained). In depression and anxiety in particular, there is a tendency to focus in on what we do not have – peace, loving spouse, sufficient finances – and miss what God has provided. The obsessive-compulsive person becomes so focused on their rituals to avoid feeling anxiety that they miss what God has given them and end up losing even more. The counselor seeks to bring to mind this enlarged focus – not just what you have lost which may genuinely be hurtful – but what you still have. You have eternal life in Christ, you have forgiveness of sin, you have a Friend who will continue with you even if everyone else walks away. You must balance your losses by looking at the overwhelming eternal benefits you have, 'who has blessed us in the heavenly realms with every spiritual blessing in Christ' (Eph. 1:3).

Those blessings do not always appear to be such to us, God's discipline itself is a blessing that proves his love to us, Hebrews 12:5–6. Christian and Faithful experience the coming of a 'Shining One' who chastises them for listening to the Flatterers:

> He chastised them sore, to teach them the good way wherein
> they should walk; and as he chastised them he said, As many
> as I love I rebuke and chasten; be zealous, therefore, and repent.
> This done, he bids them go on their way, and take good heed to the
> other directions of the Shepherds. So they thanked him for all his
> kindness and went softly along the right way, singing.

In the midst of our struggles can we accept those times when God is also disciplining us and see them as his kindness? Often we do not and once again we may need the help to see these as times we do not enjoy but which truly are beneficial as God uses the discipline to bring us back upon the correct path and save us from future suffering and trial, to save us from more time in Giant Despair's castle or worse fates.

There are numerous other dangers to consider in the process of counseling with hurting people. In speaking to Ignorance, Christian hears him state 'I will never believe that my heart is thus bad.' To which Christian replies, 'the Word of God says, that man's ways are crooked ways, not good but perverse; it says, they are naturally out of the good way, that they have not known it. Now when a man thus thinks of his ways, I say when he does sensibly, and with heart-humiliation, thus think, then has he good thoughts of his own ways because his thoughts now agree with the judgment of the word of God.' Christian warns people here of falling into the trap of modern day humanistic thinking which believes we are basically good people who sometimes do wrong things. The truth is we are sinners, who may not do the worst we could but will be unable, apart from Christ's power, to do right. Thus we must stay dependent upon and in communion with him. Too often in times of struggle people end up on one extreme or another; either all they focus on is their failure or sin and respond as if God cannot help them for they are so wicked, or they see their sin as a small failure that is not indicative of who they are at the core of their being. When this is true, they will not focus on having God bring about deep heart change in their life but rather just try to clean up the surface a bit. Christian warns us to accurately see who we are before God, so we can truly become who we should be in Christ. Later they recognize this from another perspective, that of conscience.

> Though the consciences of such men are awakened, yet their minds are not changed: therefore, when the power of guilt wear away, that which provokes them to be religious ceases; wherefore they naturally return to their own course again…so then it comes to pass, that when their guilt and fear is gone, their desires for heaven and happiness die, and they return to their course again.

The conscience is only effective if we allow it to truly prod us to recognize our guilt and then act upon that guilt in repentance to seek spiritual growth through our guilt.

THE JOURNEY'S END

Finally, the journey ends as Faithful and Christian cross the final river, Death, to find themselves in the Celestial City. Obviously, those we seek to help have not yet reached this step in the journey through life. The hope is, however, that by walking them through the journey of Christian they will be able to see their own current struggles in light of that journey, taking the steps and achieving the growth they need now to help them, not finish the journey today, but prepare for the next stage of the journey. All of us are in this journey whether we want to be or not, the question becomes whether we will pursue it in an alert, intentional manner or just follow the 'wind and tide.' A good counselor helps others become intentional in making this difficult stage of their journey one that keeps them on the right path and helps prepare them for future stages, while also trying to encourage and support them through this difficult stretch. Throughout history there has been no other book apart from the Bible, that has helped so many to continue in the journey of the Christian life as *Pilgrim's Progress*.

6

I JUST NEED TO STOP FEELING, CORRECT?

Emotions in the Christian Life[1]

The role of the emotions in the life of the believer has been an area of dispute throughout church history and remains one today. Yet it is an area that is essential for the counseling arena as emotions almost always have a role in the counseling problems we encounter. The disagreement encompasses four distinct concerns. First, should the believer be experiencing and freely expressing emotions as part of a normal Christian life or should our emphasis be more towards practicing control to be sure that logic and reason are not being hijacked by feelings? Secondly, should we respond differently to positive (joy, compassion, love) versus negative emotions (anger, sadness, jealousy)? Thirdly (although obviously connected to the first concern), what should the emphasis be with emotions – to stress control and even repression of feelings or to learn to understand

---

1 All quotations are from Jonathan Edwards, *The Religious Affections*, Banner of Truth Trust edition, 1997 reprint, unless otherwise indicated.

them so as to present them appropriately? Finally, does God exhibit emotions? Scripture distinctly presents God and Christ in his earthly life as having emotions but are these anthropomorphisms (attempts to describe God by using our limited human language and perceptions) or truly demonstrating that emotions are part of the makeup of the God in whose image we are to live?

We turn in this chapter to Jonathan Edwards (1703–58) who comes at the end of the great line of Puritan pastor-theologians. Unlike the authors considered thus far, Edwards lived and ministered in the United States in the Massachusetts area. His was a wide ministry encompassing pastor, missionary to the Native Americans in the area, college president, and key theological and practical writer for his time. Edwards began his ministry as pastor to a church in New York City at the age of nineteen! In 1727 he moved to Northampton Church to serve as assistant to his grandfather, Solomon Stoddard, the same year he married Sarah. Stoddard died shortly afterwards leaving Jonathan at age 25 as the pastor of the second largest church in New England. In 1750 a struggle ensued in the church regarding issues which Edwards saw as spiritual shallowness and drifting from Scripture (particularly about who could participate in communion). As a result, he was dismissed as pastor. He received invitations from many places including Scotland but went to Stockbridge, Massachusetts, then on the frontier with the Native Americans. He had long been concerned with the spiritual condition of the Native Americans and took this opportunity to minister to the small congregation of Native Americans and a few others from the town. He served there from 1751–8 at which time he accepted a call to become President of Princeton College. Unfortunately, his tenure there was short as he died after a few weeks from pneumonia contracted after he received a smallpox inoculation. He had a lifelong concern for theology but also for missions, for pastoral care, and for seeking to understand the world of God's creation. The depth of his thought and writings have provided solid foundations for theological development.

Edwards' legacy is extensive. A list of his descendants reveals many spiritual leaders. And without realizing it, many writings and discussions today are deeply indebted to the work of Edwards three hundred years ago. His theological depth and ability to thoroughly critique the events of his day, including the beginnings of the modernism with its overemphasis on reason (specifically reason as autonomous) that still stands today as we battle the same errors within the church and society. So it is fitting to look to one of the chief, if not the chief, of American theologians as we wrestle with the biblical understanding of the role of emotions in our lives.

In his *Treatise on Religious Affections*, Jonathan Edwards did not speak directly to the concerns about emotions raised above. He does, however, provide valuable foundational insights which are helpful for the debate. Edwards was presented with the dilemma of trying to evaluate the responses being observed during the revivals in New England as a result of his preaching initially and then of George Whitfield and others. The traditionalists, heavily influenced by rationalism, labeled the experiential responses as unspiritual and irrational because of the excessive emotional and behavioral responses that were associated with the supposed conversions. Speaking for this group was Charles Chauncy, an influential Boston pastor.

> True religion, Chauncy said, was primarily a matter of the mind, not the affections, and was characterized by self-control, cultural sophistication, and strict moral propriety. 'The plain truth is [that] an enlightened mind, and not raised affections, ought always to be the guide of those who call themselves men; and this, in the affairs of religion, as well as other things.'...The Christian life, therefore, together with an alleged encounter with the Spirit, must be reasonable, courteous, and not given to visible or vocal displays of emotion.[2]

Edwards on the other hand, did not see these responses as either inherently proving the falseness of the conversions or of their truthfulness either. Instead, from the perspective of examining the steps in the conversion process, Edwards sought to provide insights

---

2 Sam Storms, *Signs of the Spirit: An Interpretation of Jonathan Edwards' Religious Affections* (Wheaton: Crossway Books, 2007), 30–31.

on how to more effectively minister to new converts by helping them to see what were genuine signs of conversion and what were not. Edwards did not devalue reason in life but he did note that affections were the key to understanding the true Christian life. For Edwards, the term affections is much broader than the idea of emotions, but the Puritans certainly believed there was a place for emotions in the believer's life. The Puritans specifically wrote of the stages of the conversion process, the second of which Timothy Edwards described as 'humiliation.' George Marsden observes that this stage involves a lot of emotional disturbance, even though, once again, a non-Christian could have similar emotions. Yet, as Marsden notes, the Puritans believed that it was only by going through this emotionally harrowing stage that a person was ready for the next step of regeneration.[3]

Along with Timothy, Jonathan points out repeatedly that there is no particular emotional response that inherently indicates certainty of conversion, but he also rejects the idea that the presence of emotional responses proves there is no conversion as the opponents were arguing.

AFFECTIONS AS THE 'RUDDER' OF THE CHRISTIAN LIFE

Emotions then can be exhibited (perhaps better to say, will be) in the process of conversion for Edwards and other Puritans. But Jonathan Edwards is not primarily interested in emotions in his book, but with what he terms the affections. Affections will be crucial in the life of the believer at conversion but also should be present throughout their life. The term affections in our modern world is generally used as equivalent to emotions but it was a more comprehensive term for Edwards.

> True Religion, in great part, consists in Holy Affections. The affections are no other than the more vigorous and sensible exercises of the inclination and will of the soul. God has endued

---

3 Mark R. Talbot, 'Godly Emotions' in *a God Entranced Vision of All Things*, ed. John Piper and Justin Taylor (Wheaton: Crossway Books, 2004), 225.

the soul with two faculties: one that is that by which it is capable of perception and speculation or by which it discerns, and views, and judges of things; which is called the understanding.

Here he is referencing what most would refer to as thinking, as the cognitive functions that allow us to evaluate and develop beliefs. This would entail the rational, logical thinking that many of his opponents prized as the pinnacle of godly living. While accepting this as a part of who we are as people, Edwards recognizes there is a more comprehensive concept to express who we are. In essence, he uses affections to describe what is often referred to in Scripture as the 'heart.' The affections represents not merely a perception or view of things around us, but an actual inclination (or disinclination) from those things. He notes that it is sometimes referred to as the will because of the actions that come from that inclination, or the mind but 'they are these more vigorous and sensible exercises of this faculty that are called the affections.'

Two key insights arise from this. First, Edwards is urging us towards what is often referred to as a holistic viewpoint today. It is not that our mind (rational thought) or our will or our emotions or our conscience or any other part of our immaterial being is somehow in authority over the other parts of our being. Rather, we were created as a unified being and the very fact we speak of 'different parts' of who we are reflects the disruption that sin has brought to our being. Edwards does not look as the rationalists did, to logic and reason to be at the pinnacle with everything else subservient, rather he looks for the unifying principle that brings all parts of us together. This would be the affections. While difficult to grasp, it would be as if affections are the 'rudder' that steers the entire 'ship' of who we are as a person. So affections encompasses all these other characteristics. Edwards' chief argument will be that in true conversion, the affections will now reflect a desire or inclination, a choice steering us towards God and his glory and away from ourselves and the sin of the world. Thus affections will 'steer' the mind and the emotions, all the parts of who we are. This is why for Edwards it is ultimately to the affections that he turns to when trying to understand true Christianity, because emotions, behaviors, particular choices, or even cognitive beliefs will not in and of themselves point to true belief in Christ. It is the direction that the affections are choosing which will demonstrate that true belief.

Because Edwards is not referring to the emotions in a specific or distinct way, we must take care in applying his work to a discussion of emotions. For him, however, affections would encompass how we feel about things and specifically how those feelings then influence our process of choosing what we will do and what we will value as our priorities in day to day life. As Edwards clarifies, 'the soul does not merely perceive and view things but is in some way inclined with respect to the things it views or considers.' There is a perception but eventually that perception is fashioned into an active choice and response within the person which will then be observable through their outward behavior. The perception comes from the holistic working of our entire inner person.

Storms adds two important distinctions in interpreting Edwards. First, he distinguishes the affections from passions with the latter referring to Edwards' inclinations of the will that 'are more sudden, and whose effects on the animal spirits are move violent.' Secondly he distinguishes affections from feelings. There are definitely emotional dimensions to the affections, but the affections are more than emotions. 'Emotions can often be no more than physiological heightened states of either euphoria or fear that are unrelated to what the mind perceives as true. Affections on the other hand, are always the fruit or effect of what the mind understands and knows.'[4]

In summary, Edwards sees the internal nature of man as comprised of an ability, a 'faculty,' to think and understand, but unlike the rationalists he also posits this second part of who we are, the affections, as being of greater importance. The affections represent the entire process that brings the person to be inclined to do something. Edwards does not pit these two 'faculties' against one another in his writing, on the contrary he has a very keen sense of the holistic nature of who we are meant to be as people so that these

4 Storms, ibid, 45.

parts should be working together. He is also quite cognizant that we are fallen creatures in which sin affects our entire being so that the two faculties may not always be working in complementary form. But unlike some today, he does not see the rational thinking mind as somehow being unaffected by sin, he recognizes that our rational minds are just as distorted by sin as all other parts of our being, hence the need for a 'renewing of the mind' in Romans 12:2.

Thus the appeals today to just be rational and control your feelings misses this foundational understanding of who we are that Edwards presents, and leads to the same error he was fighting, that rationality is somehow primary to all feelings and thus the emotions must simply be interpreted by and made subservient to the powers of reason. That error was just as prevalent in his day as ours and certainly is one he is disputing in his development of the affections of the believer and their role in the godly life. Edwards is a firm believer in reason but presents it working in conjunction with the affections and for the true believer as guided by the affections. Edwards does seem to be providing a foundation for not seeing rationality as being the single highest goal of the Christian life to the exclusion of emotions or other parts of our unified person. Rather for him, affections rightly directed to and desiring God would be the goal for which we strive, and the affections then includes all other parts of our being.

In *Religious Affections*, Edwards references 1 Peter 1:8, 'though you have not seen him, you love him and even though you do not see him now, you believe in him and are filled with an inexpressible and glorious joy.' 'Peter's words, Edwards observes, reveal the spiritual state of the Christians to whom he was writing. They were under persecution – "grieved by various trials," as Peter puts it (1 Pet. 1:6) – and these trials tested the authenticity of their faith, which then manifested itself in the love and joy mentioned in verse 8. True faith, in other words, inevitably gives rise to godly desires and emotions.'[5] In trying to determine true religion, Edwards posits clearly that it will involve these godly desires, the affections, and

5 Talbot, ibid., 230.

that their presence is one sure sign of conversion and of assurance of faith as they continue in the believer's life. He notes that the Scriptures 'do everywhere place religion very much in affections such as fear, hope, love, hatred, desire, joy, sorrow, gratitude, compassion and zeal.' And godly figures throughout the Bible are pictured with these desires and the emotions that naturally arise from those desires. Speaking specifically of David and his lament Psalms, Edwards notes they were 'nothing else but the expressions and breathings of devout and holy affections penned for the use of the church of God in its public worship.' We will return to the laments later, but note that Edwards is absolutely stressing the need for believers to recognize that David's laments which deal with depression or anger or fear were intended to be sung publicly and thus to be instrumental in helping us develop more godly lives. And yet today, the tendency is to only sing praise oriented psalms and neglect the difficulties of the laments. Perhaps this is one cause of the relative shallowness of Christian experience in the western world today.

These godly emotions and desires should combine with our thinking, our beliefs, to produce a wholeness in our being. But although emotions themselves will not be the proof of conversion, Edwards is prepared to say that the absence of godly affections such as joy, love, and compassion, which certainly have an emotional element to them, indicates a heart that has not given itself to Christ. Emotions do indicate what the person is truly concerned about, revealing their spiritual condition. On the first point of controversy regarding emotions, Edwards is indirectly supportive – yes, the believer should be experiencing emotions as godly emotions can actually be a demonstration of the work of God in their heart.

CONTROL, REPRESS OR EXAMINE EMOTIONS

Because Edwards is well aware that not all emotions are necessarily godly, he next turns his attention to trying to discern true from false affections; 'having much affection [does not] prove that he has any true religion' but 'if he has not affection it proves that he has no religion' being 'in a state of spiritual death.' Having stated this truth in a doctrinal way he then proceeds to make several inferences from it. First, 'We may hence learn how great their error is who are for discarding all religious affections, as having nothing solid or substantial in them.' This reiterates his basic point already developed that we can not just discard affections as somehow being opposed to rationality and thus of no use to the believer or the person seeking to help that believer.

Rather, secondly, 'If it be so that true religion lies much in the affections, hence we may infer that such means are to be desired as have much of a tendency to move the affections.' Edwards takes the bold step (bold in the eyes of his disparagers at least) that since affections are a crucial part of the godly life then we should seek out the ways that God would have us develop these affections and ensure that they are righteous in nature. So, rather than just evaluate the emotional and experiential responses seen in others during the revivals, Edwards now moves to encouraging that we discover how to produce or grow in those very affections that his critics were potentially condemning. Applying this notion to emotions for us today, this immediately clarifies that the first goal with our inner emotions should not be to simply control them (control may be required ultimately, but is not necessarily the first response) and certainly not to repress them, but instead to seek a godly manner of examining them to make sure they are being lead by godly affections and not ungodly ones; and perhaps to be more faithful to Edwards, to ensure they are not simply feelings but are more fully engaging our heart to produce godly desires (versus self-centered desires) and action based upon those desires.

Edwards continues thirdly, 'God has given to mankind affections that they might be subservient to man's chief end, the business of religion. And yet how common is it among mankind, that their affections are much more exercised and engaged in other matters than in religion!' Here Edwards drives home his most foundational concern, whether talking about affections, thinking, or any other activity of the believer the goal should be that they are actively supporting us in our ability to live for and pursue God. Too often our surface responses seem to be focused on God, when in reality they are motivated by desires to appear good to others, or to achieve our own definitions of success, to feel good, or a myriad of other internal concerns. In these cases, we are not being led by godly affections, but rather are making deep, inner choices that are not focused upon God but upon being well seen by ourselves and others.

Although he will address the excesses and problems of the revivals and note with regret that some whom he felt were genuine converts later fell away from the faith, Edwards still wants to be sure we do not throw out the baby with the bathwater. Yes, critique and recognize the problems, but also see that too often our worship of God is mired in rational and correct belief but without the passion and desires of the person who truly understands what God has done for him in Christ (consider the church at Ephesus in Revelation 2:1–7). Or consider David, a man after God's own heart, who as King can freely dance in the streets before the Ark of God, and can also write songs of despair and frustration. Both illustrate that he is seeking to allow his passions, his emotions, to be 'exercised in religion.' Edwards could almost be speaking of our modern day dilemma of seeing believers at sporting events (myself included) impassioned and cheering (or groaning) for their team, but then when we turn to our spiritual life there is a basic deadness, even if a correct belief. The enjoyment of the sporting event is not inherently wrong but may well point to a lack of true enjoyment of God and his blessings as our chief end in life.

Edwards tries earnestly to not pit truth and theological doctrine against the affections and their response to the Christian life. Part of my own amazement with Edwards is that he is firmly committed to theological understanding in his writings, his preaching, and in the lives of his congregations. But without any hesitation he couples that theological depth with a marvelous commitment to believers experiencing passionate spiritual lives in the worship and service of their King. The two are never pitted against each other in Scripture and yet still today Christians take one or the other side and resist the effort of bringing both together. Leaving doctrine aside will lead to the shallowness of belief and life that Edwards is always fervently fighting in his ministry. Emphasizing doctrine to the exclusion of worship and passion in the Christian life will lead to sterile ministry that becomes more and more built upon intellectual understanding alone. For Edwards it is both/and, not either/or, as there is no actual dichotomy as is too often made today by believers who do not grasp that doctrine is actually about worship of God. It is not simply that right doctrine leads to worship of God, but that doctrine as understanding of God and his works is itself worship. And worship certainly should be passionate because worship is about the wonders of our God and his salvation for us.

LAMENTS AS A MODEL

Edwards complements well the work of Dan Allender and Tremper Longman, III in their book, *The Cry of the Soul*, and more recently that of Michael Card in *A Sacred Sorrow* (see also Carl Trueman's chapter on the Psalms in *The Wages of Spin*). Both of these books specifically focus on the emotions yet you sense this is for the sake of simplicity as both books are urging us to an even deeper heart change than is entailed simply by the change of emotions. Both books challenge us to first examine our emotions, to hear what they are saying about what we believe about God, the world, and ourselves. They focus on the laments in Scripture as specific examples of how godly people accomplish this process. The Psalms in particular demonstrate that we should listen to this inner voice of the emotions, 'Why, O my soul are you in despair?' (Ps. 42:11). With Edwards, they agree that the desires and feelings, the inclinations of our inner heart, are often indicative of our spiritual state. As such they should not be simply ignored, repressed or subjected immediately to control, but instead be listened to as a source of understanding of who we are at that moment. Is the goal to just yield to the emotions as inherently correct biblically? No, for this would fall into the opposite trap that Edwards was also writing against – those who immediately assumed that the emotional responses seen in the revivals were automatically indicators of God at work in the person. Edwards knew too well that many who started well later dropped off from the faith, thus their emotional responses were not definite indicators of God's work in their lives. Edwards was also repeatedly stating how unbelievers have strong affections that may be similar to or even be counterfeits of real godly affections. There are always examples of those who do not follow Christ, being sacrificial in service to others and seeming to demonstrate deep love for others, and yet their outwardly good actions ultimately fall short as they are not for the glory of God. Gandhi is a twentieth century example of this. His life, which accomplished so much good, ultimately fell short before God because he was not inclined to follow the one true God and Christ as the ultimate commitment in his life.

Thus emotions are not simply to be heeded and allowed to determine our response because they are present. Edwards notes how some argue that a thought or feeling arose that was not of their own doing (at least they do not think it is) and so it must be from the working of the Spirit of God. He responds, 'what they have been the subjects of may indeed not be from themselves directly, but may be from the operation of an invisible agent, some spirit besides their own: but it does not thence follow that it was from the Spirit of God.' There are other spirits besides the Holy Spirit which is why we are directed to test the spirits to see if they are of God. 'As a person who is asleep has dreams that he is not the voluntary author of; so may such persons in like manner be the subjects of involuntary impressions when they are awake.'

Experiences and feelings do not automatically equate to being from God. But they should not be ignored out of hand. For Edwards, to do so, would fail to 'try the spirits' and would negate the last portion of his book in which he tries to examine the affections to see where they are helpful to us and where they are not. To just push them aside would also miss 'the cry of the soul' which is telling us how we understand what is happening to us. That understanding may be incorrect as it was with David's laments when he claimed that God was not being faithful to him, but it is in hearing those understandings that David was able to return to a deepened faith in God in his time of trial.

Allender and Longman challenge that looking inside is not for the purpose of trying to change 'negative' emotions into 'positive' ones. Rather, we need to 'listen' to what we feel in order to understand what our emotions are telling us about how we are viewing the world around us and particularly a mysterious God who does not act in the ways we might expect him to. They also note that behavioral techniques to control emotions will always fall short. Certainly, we should pray but in the end we should pursue 'wrestling' with God through our emotions in order to experience deeper growth in our spiritual life. The wrestling that we see David, Jeremiah, and Job engage in results in a deepening of faith in a God and world that do not always make sense to us, and in the laments it results in a renewed statement of faith and worship in God (except for Psalm 88), an expression of the desire and emotion of joy that we so much prefer to see. But that expression comes through the experience of the wrestling, not apart from it!

EXAMINATION AS A PRIORITY IN THE CHRISTIAN LIFE

> The affections also function like a watermark, when examined they reveal our true identity. And holding up the affections to the light becomes Edwards's primary concern in Religious Affections.... Edwards here stresses a crucial element of Puritanism: examination. Bunyan, Edwards, and other Puritans were intent on examining both their own lives, due to the powers of self-deception, and the lives of others, due to the subtleties of hypocrisy.[6]

A proper biblical examination, guided by the Spirit (Ps. 139:23–4) is a vital discipline in the believer's life. 2 Corinthians 13:5 is one of many passages that directly challenge believers to examine their lives. Edwards and other Puritan writers, have left this legacy of the importance of self-examination. For them it is not a morbid, introspective look into ourselves to try to find as much 'dirt' as we can. Rather, it is based on their healthy fear of self-deception. They

---

6 Stephen J. Nichols, *Jonathan Edwards: a Guided Tour of His life and Thought* (Phillipsburg, NJ: P&R Press, 2001), 114–15.

realized how easy it is for us to see ourselves as better than who we really are, or as having pure motives when in reality they are mixed at best. The twin problem with the revivals was that the detractors only examined the affections from a purely rational standpoint, resulting in a faulty judgment, while many on the other side did no examination at all, simply claiming I experienced it therefore it must be true. The laments in Scripture serve as a model for how godly people through the ages engaged in self-examination by in essence directing that examination towards God, being brutally honest in what they saw or felt in themselves, but always keeping the process under the direction of God through the indwelling Spirit and the written Word of God. In counseling, many wish only for surface changes and when those occur we may celebrate 'successful' counseling when in reality we may be leaving the person in the same position as many of those in Edwards' day who had incredible experiences during the revivals, assumed they were evidence of God at work, did no self-examination in light of Scripture, and later drifted away because their affections had not been truly changed from a focus upon self and the world to a new desire to pursue after God. We would do well to model Edwards' careful examination in helping those we counsel, as well as in our own spiritual lives.

POSITIVE OR NEGATIVE EMOTIONS

Although not the focus of his book, Edwards clearly understands this struggle with positive versus negative emotions from the perspective of the affections as he describes the affections of being of two kinds, those by which the soul desires to cleave to or seek after and those to which it is opposed. 'Of the former sort are love, desire, hope, joy gratitude, complacence. Of the latter kind are hatred, fear, anger, grief, and such like.' Edwards realizes that both sorts of affections (and therefore emotions as a part of the affections) are present within us and both can be proper. It is not the idea of being 'positive' or 'negative' in nature that identifies a godly desire or emotion for Edwards. A desire or emotion is right when it is appropriate to the context a person is in. A person who has just learned of the sudden death of a loved one, probably should be experiencing some 'negative' emotion(s) or we would assume there is something wrong with them.

There are two situations we face – first, we may have negative emotions that are not truly godly but are present and simply willing them away will not work (see Allender & Longman); and secondly negative emotions can be correct when they are responding accurately to the context of living in a fallen world. They involve our reaction against something that has occurred so that we feel dislike, disapproval, or perhaps anger at injustice. It would be wonderful if we only experienced positive desires and emotions, but as Talbot describes, the same reactions that produce positive emotions 'when we have certain beliefs will inevitably give rise to negative emotions when we have other beliefs. If I am able to feel joy at my wedding, then I am also capable of feeling sorrow if something bad happens to my wife.'[7]

Scripture illustrates this in passages that proclaim 'Let those who love the Lord, hate evil!' (Ps. 97:10, see Amos 5:15, Rom. 12:9, 2 Chron. 19:2). And David actually appeals to his hatred as proof of a godly heart, 'I abhor the assembly of evildoers, and refuse to sit with the wicked' (Ps. 26:5), or Psalm 31:6 in which he proclaims hatred not just to evil but to the people who worship idols. As Edwards notes, Christians 'are called upon to give evidence of their sincerity by this, "You that love the Lord, hate evil."' Similarly, Psalm 139:17–24 should cause us to stop and reflect upon that often heard cliché, 'love the sinner and hate the sin' and ask whether this statement truly is reflective of the biblical language or whether it is yet another effort to resolve simplistically the dilemma of the affections demonstrated to us by God in his nature (Deut. 12:31, 16:22; Prov. 6:16–18; Isa. 1:14, 61:8; Ps. 5:5, 11:5; Hosea 9:15)? The words love and hate can be understood better by seeing them through this lens of the affections, they reflect where our inclinations point and also stress that true godly affections are fully focused upon God or not upon God.

7 Talbot, 243.

WHAT OF THE EMOTIONS OF GOD?

This is not a subject matter for Edwards in *Religious Affections*. Suffice it to say, that it is implicit in his argument that Christ manifested the affections he speaks of, albeit always in their perfect, sinless state. B. B. Warfield states it as an obvious truth –

> It belongs to the truth of our Lord's humanity, that he was subject to all sinless human emotions. In the accounts which the Evangelists give us of the crowded activities which filled the few years of his ministry, the play of a great variety of emotions is depicted. It has nevertheless not proved easy to form a universally acceptable conception of our Lord's emotional life.[8]

For the sake of simplicity here, I would suggest the conclusion that Scripture presents both God and Christ as having genuine emotions that we are to reflect because we are made in the image of God. A perusal of the New Testament will quickly reveal examples of the emotions of Christ (for further development see Warfield's complete article or *Faithful Feelings* by Matthew Elliott):

- Compassion (Mark 1:40–41, Luke 7:13, Mark 8:2, Matt. 9:36).
- Anger (Mark 3:5, he was angry and grieved, Mark 10:14, John 2:14–17).
- Grief (Luke 19:41–4, John 11:33–5, John 13:21, Matt. 26:38, Isa. 53:4).
- Joy (Luke 10:21–4, John 15:11, 17:13).
- Love (Luke 22:15, Mark. 10:21, John 11:3, John 15:12–14).

WHAT SHOULD WE DO WITH THESE EMOTIONS?

As Edwards examines the affections relative to whether they truly represent a work of God or not, he reminds us that the emotions

---

8 B. B. Warfield, 'The Emotional Life of our Lord', from *Biblical and Theological Studies*. (New York: Charles Scribner's Sons, 1912). from website, http://www.the-highway.com/ emotion-Christ_Warfield.html.

(and all other parts of our being) are not amoral – they do have a moral quality about them. So we do not want to accept the position of some portions of modern culture which state that what you feel is ok, period. Just express them and do not think about them. On the contrary, emotions are affected by sin just like all other parts of our being and so they are dealing with moral issues. It is not that we should simply accept them as felt and express them. Remember again that Edwards' desire is not to see cognitive, rational thought as somehow predominant and controlling of the affections but neither does he just accept the affections as being godly because they occurred in the midst of a religious revival. Rather, he challenges us that our beliefs and affections should be working together to complement and inform each other. And in a long section in his book he seeks to explore how to tell if affections are godly in nature or not – do they flow from an understanding of Scripture as one example. If not, then they are certainly questionable. 'Holy affections are not heat without light; but ever more arise from the information of the understanding, some spiritual instruction that the mind receives; some light or actual knowledge.' Believers will be 'affected' because they are either having their understanding of divine things deepened in the sense of new understandings or the mind renewed in areas that sin had distorted it previously (1 John 4:7, Phil. 1:9, Rom. 10:2, Col. 3:10). But there are also affections that do not arise from this 'light in the understanding.' If Scripture is the source of the light or the 'heart's burning with gracious affection' as it was with the disciples in Luke 24:32, then it is a godly source. Affections and all their components – will, emotions, desire, belief, must in the end arise from the work of Scripture in our lives and therefore be compatible with Scripture in their actual outworking.

As noted earlier, numerous authors have noticed the power of the laments to help us in this area of seeking to experience and practice godly emotions. Song writer Michael Card asks several questions, 'Isn't it wrong to complain by lamenting to God? Is it not a sign of rebellion and faithlessness? How can it be appropriate to show my anger to him?' He agrees that these are all just questions. But he then points to the fact that God has provided us with many laments in the Word of God. Why would they be there if not to help us learn how to engage in this struggle in our lives. 'People like Job, David, Jeremiah, and even Jesus reveal to us that prayers of complaint can still be prayers of faith. They represent the last refusal to let go of the God who may seem to be absent or worse – uncaring.' Laments are not denials of our faith but honest efforts to hold onto our faith in the face of events we do not understand, to wrestle with a gracious God who is willing to hear our deepest struggles as an act of worship of him as the only one who can respond to those struggles.[9]

This raises a crucial question analogous to Edwards' dilemma as to who was truly converted and who was not – how do the laments differ from the grumblers in the wilderness? God destroyed those who grumbled in Israel's desert wanderings, but he spared and heard those who offered laments. At least two differences are readily apparent. First, grumbling turns to God with accusations that are statements that do not look for a response and have no expectation that God will respond or work, while the laments come to God with complaints that seem to have a question mark at the end and are looking to and expecting God to both respond and act. Second, laments approach God directly, while the grumbler's complaints go to a third person rather than being directed to God. In other words, the laments demonstrate struggle and complaint but also faith in God, for they are still turning to God even in the midst of complaint saying this is how it feels but I refuse to let go of my belief in you and so I seek your help with my conflict. In Edwards' terms, they reflect an understanding of what they know to be true but recognize this understanding is in conflict with what they feel but since their desire is to honor God, they bring the struggle to him for resolution. For the grumblers there is no longer any expression of faith in God, rather there is a statement of God's irrelevance and their own refusal to even consider that he may have a resolution for their complaint. Thus laments serve believers of all ages as a model for how to wrestle through their inner emotions so

---

9 Michael Card, *A Sacred Sorrow: Reaching Out to God in the Lost Language of Lament* (Colorado Springs: NavPress, 2005), 17, 30–31.

as to have those emotions direct them to deeper faith rather than away from God (the grumblers) or to a shallow, feeling-less faith (of the stoics or overly rational approaches). Edwards seems to appreciate this process based on his notation of the importance of David's struggles as presented for the public worship of believers. In essence, it would be one of the biblical methodologies he might endorse for developing truly godly affections that do have a day to day effect in the 'religious' life of the individual.

HOW THEN DO WE WORK WITH OUR TROUBLESOME EMOTIONS?

Having worked through the basic concerns in the disagreements about emotions, it still remains to ask how those in counseling settings can be helped to develop the genuinely godly emotions and even more so the affections that Edwards sought out in the new converts of his day. It is hard to engage in counseling without emotions coming into focus at some point whether in the obvious cases of people struggling with grief or depression or anger or jealousy or even love (should I marry this person whom I feel love for?), or less obviously as factors involved in how to make an important decision or how to seek a job or how to try to resolve a conflict. Unfortunately, because emotions are so often either discounted or encouraged without comment in the evangelical church, there has been a lack of consistent training and thus there is a lack of the theological foundation that Edwards brings to the discussion. For example, many sermons and bible studies on anger have begun by quoting Ephesians 4:26, 'in your anger do not sin,' but then they typically turn rapidly to talk about unrighteous anger and its consequences in our lives. The result is that hearers are told that there is righteous anger but usually walk away with no notion of what it might look like, when it should be exercised, or how to tell the difference from unrighteous anger. Over time, the message seems to become that all anger is unrighteous since that is what the bulk of the teaching is concerned with. This then perpetuates the positive versus negative emotion error with anger being perceived as a negative emotion and thus one that should always be controlled away. Those with anger struggles will often arrive in counseling situations without a balanced view that anger might actually be righteous. They would prefer the anger to just be removed (and in fairness usually their anger is unrighteous in nature) but this can not be the starting place as it would leave them without any sense of how to be angry in the right ways.

So how might we help those we counsel to start the process of trying to wrestle with their emotions so that they may become reflective of God and his work in their lives? First, they should be encouraged not to deny what they are feeling, especially as emotions can not simply be turned off. Denial leaves the emotions at work but in an undirected way. Far better to recognize the emotions so they can enter into the intentional process that Edwards demonstrates in Religious Affections. He was quite methodical in trying to evaluate affections to see if they were godly in nature and the same rigor can be applied to the emotions, which can be viewed as a subset of the affections. Recognizing and feeling the emotions is the best starting place for deciding how to wrestle with God. Lamentations 3 is a direct example of this process. Most of us are familiar with verses 22 and 23, 'your compassions are new every morning, great is your faithfulness.' The hymn, 'Great is Thy Faithfulness' is taken from this passage. It is an incredible hymn of testimony to God's faithfulness, but what most singers do not realize is the context that those verses are found in. Lamentations describes the horrible siege with accompanying famine, and destruction of Jerusalem during Jeremiah's lifetime. In chapter 3, Jeremiah describes how he feels as he sits in the burning ruins of the city, surrounded by dead bodies and feeling the physical effects of the famine in his own body. As you read through those first 21 verses they are hardly uplifting, on the contrary they are quite depressing and speak of God in ways that make us distinctly uncomfortable, such as describing him like a lion that jumps out, mauls us and is not even kind enough to finish us off, but rather leaves us laying in the road maimed but not dead (vv. 10–11).

Eventually Jeremiah follows the pattern of lament and returns to God as his source of Hope in the midst of the crisis. But Jeremiah reached that tremendous statement of God's faithfulness by first going through those twenty-one verses, he did not start with verses 22–3. Too often, we seek to have strugglers start with verses 22–3 and thereby deny them the reality of the struggle with God that produces deep faith responses such as Jeremiah's. Is it any wonder that people turn away from the faith in times of struggle if we offer them true but simplistic platitudes that are not consistent with the Scriptural record? Taking people through the first 21 verses will result in the deepening of faith, the transformation of the person evidenced in verses 22–3.

> All gracious affections do arise from a spiritual understanding, in which the soul has the excellency and glory of divine things discovered to it, as was shown before. But all spiritual discoveries are transforming, and not only make an alteration of the present exercise, sensation, and frame of the soul; but such power and efficacy have they, that they make an alteration in the very nature of the soul: 2 Corinthians 3:18.

Similarly, even the Lord Jesus demonstrates the lament model in his struggle in the Garden of Gethsemane (Luke 22:39–46). The language of the text is pointedly describing the anguish he felt as he reflected on what it would mean to drink the cup of God's wrath, to take all of the sin of the world upon himself. It is significant to the nature of being human that he asked not once but three times if there was any other way but to drink this cup. I suspect we would expect him to ask once and then turn to do the will of God. He does accept and follow the will of God but only after asking three times. If he could engage with God in that way, how much more should we as sinful human beings in our times of struggle. Yes, in the end it is crucial that the 'inclination' is to honor and follow God as it was with Christ but the act of wrestling is part of how that 'inclination' brings our desires and our feelings into accord with those of God.

Secondly, we do want to recognize the limitations of emotions. They are only part of our being. For Edwards they are not even the total sum of what he intends by the word affections (and what Scripture entails by the 'heart'). As such we can too easily allow emotions to be the only source for evaluating what we believe. Emotions are influenced by the events we are experiencing and our perception of those events. Our perception while real to us may or may not be accurate to reality because we are always limited, not being able to see as God sees. The goal then becomes as Edwards stressed, to seek to have our emotions function as part of the inner affections and have that work with our rational thinking so that we will be functioning as a unity which is striving to be fully focused upon God and serving and loving him. Ignoring of any part of our being can result in a wrong perception and thus a wrong response.

Edwards is quick to point out that love is the ultimate expression of godly affections and in this sense all emotions are to be conditioned by love. 'And it is true that nothing is more excellent, heavenly, and divine, than a spirit of true Christian love to God and men. It is the chief of the graces of God's Spirit, and the life, essence and sum of all true religion.' Not only is love the preeminent affection (and emotion and action) but love also reflects that our ultimate focus is not on how we feel or want to respond, rather we are to focus on how to love God and others. Self-love does not produce godly affections for self-love is naturally present in us and even in the demons. Luke 6:32 points out that love of others from selfish motives is present in all people, the wicked included. Believers should arrive at love differently, 'They do not first see that God loves them, and then see that he is lovely, but they first see that God is lovely, and that Christ is excellent and glorious, and then, consequentially, they see God's love, and great favor to them.' Believers begin with God, and self-love should be only secondary in the sense that there are true benefits for me in loving God, but the primary ground for loving God should always be who God is in his person, regardless of any personal benefits he may provide to me. False affections 'begin with self, and an acknowledgment of an excellency in God, and an affectedness with it, is only consequential and dependent.'

Emotions are not simply to be 'freely expressed' or 'dumped' upon others but should be wrestled with not only to help us understand what they say about our spiritual state but also so as to understand how to express them in ways that seek to love God and love our neighbor. Even with dealing with the crucial task of defending biblical truth from false teachers, Paul still commands us to 'speak the truth in love' (Eph. 4:15, 1 Cor. 13). So emotions, as every other part of our being, should be conditioned by love in their expression and out working.

Finally, a question of importance in counseling relates to how to respond when our feelings seem to be contrary to correct biblical action. Although it is always important to help the person wrestle through the emotions to understand what they are expressing about their heart, it is also true that we can not wait for right feelings to drive us to action. At times, the correct biblical action is clear-cut and the person needs to be encouraged to try to take the step as an act of the will and their beliefs. At times our emotions will lead us quickly and easily into the correct actions (consistent godly affections) while at other times they may be fighting against our beliefs and understandings. The biblical idea of loving your enemies (Matt. 5:43–4, Rom. 12:14–21) illustrates this difference. It is unlikely that when we first realize that we are called upon to love an enemy, that we do so with feelings of love or compassion. More likely we have thoughts of praying for lightning bolts to strike them! But as we seek to practice biblical love appropriate to who they are we often find our ability to feel mercy and compassion increases. In this instance, we are bringing our inner feelings into line with our belief in loving our enemy and the act of our will and desire to actually practice love towards them.

Ultimately, we hope to achieve the goal of having inner feelings of love and compassion towards our enemies just as God did towards us (Rom. 5:8). Edwards describes how 'gracious affections' will be attended with the 'lamb-like, love-like spirit and temper of Jesus Christ. In other words, they naturally beget and promote such a spirit of love, meekness, quietness, forgiveness and mercy, as appeared in Christ.' In his observation, 'gracious affections' will soften the heart resulting in the Christ-like spirit, while 'false affections' although initially presenting with a melting of the heart, will eventually result in hardening of the heart. As a believer loves God, the more he desires to love him, and the more uneasy is he at his want of love to him; the more he hates sin, the more he desires to hate it, and laments that he has so much remaining love to it.'

In closing, I would offer this summary of the true signs of religious affections at work in the light of the believer. We have demonstrated the importance of working with the emotions of strugglers to help them seek to grow to be more like Christ in what they feel and how they respond to those feelings. But lest we misconstrue Edwards, it is also important to recognize the larger category of affections to make sure that our goal does not simply become trying to help others feel more biblically, but more so help them to live out the affections that are truly godly and demonstrate the working of God in their life versus those affections that any person may be able to exhibit even apart from the working of God's spirit in their life. Stephen Nichols helpfully summarizes the latter argument of Edwards' book as he works to demonstrate what are and what are not signs of genuine religious affections. Many times those in counseling will demonstrate characteristics from the left column which cause them to appear spiritual to themselves or others, but the true reality is revealed by Edwards' 'Certain Signs' in the right column below. As just one example, 'talking about religion' (#3) may occur in a person who while going to church and even studying Scripture has not truly decided to embrace Scripture as the authority and guide in his life, let alone as a wonderful gift from God to them. They would demonstrate the uncertain sign of talking about the Christian life but not be demonstrating a deep, inner love for Christianity and willingness to allow the truths of Christ to guide all of his life. Assessing which column the person is truly in can help tremendously in knowing how to help them proceed with their growth:

SIGNS OF GENUINE RELIGIOUS AFFECTIONS[10]

No Certain Signs	*Certain Signs*
1 Great deal of religious zeal or fervor	Genuine source: the affections are spiritual, supernatural, and divine
2 Effects on the body (physical manifestations)	Delight in divine things not for self-interest
3 Talking about religion	Love of divine things for their inherent beauty & excellency
4 Source other than self	Illumination: rightly understanding divine things
5 Ability to recite Scripture	Assurance: conviction of the reality and certainty of divine Things
6 The appearance of love	Humiliation: a sense of insufficiency and unworthiness
7 Multiple and various affections	Transformation: change of nature
8 Affections follow a pattern	Christ-likeness: promote love, meekness, quietness, forgiveness, and mercy, as well as boldness & zeal
9 Devoting much time to religion and zealous	Sensitivity: a tender, not a hardened heart in worship
10 Praising & glorifying God in speech	Symmetry and proportion: reflecting whole image of Christ, not a disproportion of the affections
11 Self-confidence in religious experience	Spiritual hunger: desiring the self and sin less and spiritual Growth more
12 Outward signs that convince even the saints	Bearing fruit: the manifestation of Christianity as the Business of life

10 Stephen J. Nichols, ibid., p. 117.

7

HOW CAN I FIND JOY AGAIN?

Finding the Way Through Depression[1]

Depression has become a familiar condition in our modern world. Not that it had been uncommon in the past; a reading of the Old Testament reveals many struggling with symptoms of what we today would label as depression – Moses (Exod. 2:14–22), Elijah (1 Kings 19), David (repeatedly in his Psalms such as 42:11), other Psalmists, and Jeremiah (Lam. 3). Depressive symptoms exist in descriptions of historical figures throughout the ages as well. Today, however, not only will the average believer find themselves face to face with depressed people in their own church, but even television advertisements for anti-depressants occur frequently during prime time television periods. So, is depression more prevalent today? Probably not, although it would be difficult to truly measure. But it certainly is more public, more talked about than in earlier periods of history.

---

1 All quotations in this chapter are from William Bridge, *A Lifting up for the Downcast*, Banner of Truth edition, 2001 reprint, unless otherwise indicated.

Not surprisingly, since depression is as old as time, the Puritan writers did recognize it as a pastoral problem and sought to help their people struggle with it in biblical ways (it was referred to as discouragement or in more severe occurrences as melancholy). William Bridge's *A Lifting Up for the Downcast* is a collection of thirteen sermons he preached on the subject (at Stepney Church in London, 1648) from the text of Psalm 42:11. He clearly recognized that the people he ministered to became discouraged and fell into despair because of their difficult life conditions. And it should be noted that living conditions in England in the 1600s were consistently more difficult than the majority of Americans will ever face! The people knew despair and hopelessness all too well from overcrowding, lack of employment, poverty, disease, threat of war, threat of religious persecution, and poor sanitary situations.

William Bridge was born in 1600 and graduated from Emmanuel College, Cambridge in 1626. After that, he was a pastor in two different locations until being forced out of the country in 1637 during the Laudian persecutions. He fled to Holland where he pastored with Jeremiah Burroughs in Rotterdam. In 1642, he returned to England along with other persecuted Puritans. He become pastor in Great Yarmouth, while also preaching at times to Parliament and serving with the Westminster Assembly. But with the Act of Conformity in 1662 he was once again forced out of his church. He continued preaching where he could until his death in 1670. He was known as a scholar, a student, an excellent preacher, and a man who was concerned for people.

Bridge simply accepts the presence of discouragement and despair in the lives of believers without taking the time to talk about whether it should be present or not. This is one of those seemingly simple questions which require a complex answer. Is it acceptable for Christians to be depressed? The answer is Yes and No. No, in the sense that if we fully understood God and what he has and is doing for us, we would be encouraged daily to persevere through this life to our promised glorified life in eternity. We would be saddened by the effects of sin and injustice in this fallen world but not discouraged because we would be conscious of God's ever present work and the future glory awaiting us. But the answer would also be Yes, if we recognize that living in a fallen world means that none of us achieves perfect faith in God this side of heaven. So we do become discouraged and depressed at times because of our own sins or our struggle to experience God in the midst of our struggles. We live in a sinful world that does not 'work' correctly because of the general effects of sin. We see starving children, war, famine, drought, abuse, and so many other evils resulting from sin which should bring some degree of discouragement at the terrible suffering that sin brings into the world. And it is also a Yes if we recognize that depressive feelings are a common struggle for the majority of believers (at differing levels of intensity and length) whether they should be or not! As a typical struggle we must be prepared to provide biblical guidance on how to wrestle through this at times, life debilitating condition.

FOUNDATIONAL TRUTH REGARDING DEPRESSION

Beginning his commentary on Psalm 42:11 Bridge notes two remedies that David utilizes in working with his own discouragements – 'self-reprehension and self-admonition.' This seems an unlikely starting point since depressed people usually are already negative about themselves and their lives. Bridge, however, is pointing to a deeper understanding on David's part of how the condition of depression reveals his spiritual life. David challenges himself for his distrust of a God who has proved himself trustworthy over and over in his life. Then he calls upon himself to exercise faith by waiting upon God for his answer in his time. In this, David points us to the obvious answer to depression – trust in the God who is in control and has proved his love and care already at the Cross – albeit a difficult answer to take hold of! This verse leads to several implicit understandings.

> First, that there is an inward peace of the soul, which the saints and people of God ordinarily are endued with. Secondly, it is possible that this peace may be interrupted, and God's people may be much discouraged, and cast down. Thirdly, that the saints and people of God have no reason for their discouragements whatever their condition may be.

Here Bridge demonstrates the Puritan reliance on the truths of
Scripture combined with a practical ministry of caring for people.
Believers have no reason for depression. If he stopped there, then
the common accusation that the Puritans place more of a burden
on strugglers might be accurate. But he does not stop, he notes that
godly people do become discouraged and lose sight of the peace of
God that they should be experiencing (Phil. 4:7, 9).

By providing this biblical truth at the outset, Bridge provides
a foundation for ministry to those who are struggling with depression
while coupling it with a tender care that does not simply 'bash' them
with lack of faith but recognizes their genuine and real struggles
and seeks to bring them back to the true foundations of their faith.
He also 'normalizes' the struggle by recognizing its presence in
many believers, even the godly such as David, and further points
the depressed back to God as the one to help them. Overcoming
depression is not about a stoic, 'pull yourself up by the bootstraps'
type of approach. The inward peace of the soul is 'endued' by God to
individual believers. We do not make it happen or even find it through
some diligent search, rather as we seek and experience God in our
daily lives, it is a peace that he provides to us, 'the peace of God.' That
it is a supernatural peace, not something found in this natural world
or in our own personal efforts, is also stressed, 'the peace of God,
which transcends all understanding.' It is a peace that is beyond our
ability to understand in terms of its being present in difficulties or in
terms of looking at the seemingly unexplainable evils around us in
this world.

THE NECESSITY OF COMFORT

Turning to another group of discouraged believers, Bridge comments
on Isaiah 40:1. This passage was written especially to be read later in
history by the Israelites who had been taken away from their land
into captivity in Babylon. While there they began to wonder if God
had forgotten them and if he would ever return them to their land.
Writing 150 years before their time, Isaiah speaks to this group of
discouraged people and as Bridge states 'God has commanded us to

comfort, and comfort twice, "Comfort you, Comfort you," not once, but twice.' Comforting strugglers is a crucial aspect for effective counseling with any struggling person. But there are different types of comforters, as he takes note of Job's three friends who 'speak hard words unto poor distressed souls. Well, says God, therefore, in verse 2, "Speak you comfortably" [NIV 'tenderly'].' We can and must bring the foundational truths from Scripture to those who are struggling but it must be done in a truly comforting, supporting manner. This theme is also echoed in Isaiah 42:2–3 which describes the Servant of God (a reference to Christ in his incarnation) as gentle, and not breaking the bruised reed (the Puritan, Richard Sibbes, wrote *The Bruised Reed*, on this passage of Scripture). Too often counselors swing to extremes in this area. They feel that bringing truth about sin and sinful responses, or the need to deepen faith, to a depressed person is uncaring and so they avoid the subject. To the other extreme, some just say you need to 'snap out of it, start doing the right things, and trust God.' Bridge steers us down the middle of these two extremes – emphasizing the role of comfort and support while also bringing them to the truths of Scripture as the only effective way of battling their depression. He further adds that some are so discouraged that they have difficulty hearing the words of comfort that are brought to them. In that case, those who minister should 'lift up your voice and cry: not only speak to the heart, but cry, lift up your voice.' He does not intend here to yell at them, but is emphasizing the need to be insistent and seeking to make the voice of Scripture heard through the discouraging inner voice of their depressive feelings. It is not enough to only comfort them because the genuine comforting must include helping them sort out truth from unreality, as well as assisting them to grow in their spiritual maturity. This is accomplished by helping them find and grasp the relevant truths of Scripture through the fog of their depression.

A key characteristic of an effective counselor is the ability to enter into the world of the struggler and understand how they are seeing the world around them. This is not done simply to validate the feelings of the struggler, as they may be incorrect at times, but in order to determine how to keep this balance of bringing truth while also bringing comfort in their distress. We must seek to understand the world of the person who has had long struggles with depression. Many have struggled with depression on a consistent (and sometimes constant) basis for two, four, ten years or more and have limited experience of the peace of God which is promised in Scripture. How can this be if they truly know Christ as their Savior? 'You must know that there is a fundamental peace which the saints and people of God have; and there is an additional peace. A fundamental peace, which naturally arises and flows from their justification (Rom. 5:1). And then there is an additional peace, which arises from the sense of their justification. Possibly a child of God may for a long time lose the latter, but the former he shall never lose. As a woman that has a great property, takes a journey, and meets with thieves, and they take away all the money that she has about her, but yet, says she, though they have taken away my spending money, they cannot take away my inheritance.' Being free of judgment for our sin, 'no condemnation for those who are in Christ Jesus' (Rom. 8:1), establishes the basis for peace with God. He is no longer the Judge who must punish us but instead becomes the loving Father who adopts us as his children (He will still discipline us as needed but in love for the purpose of growth). This is the fundamental peace that is for every believer. But do we always feel that peace in day to day life? No, events and experiences take us away temporarily from the peace we now have with God through Christ. But a person can certainly find themselves in this position and still truly be a believer in Christ.

PEACE IN DEPRESSION

Too often modern believers believe that being a Christian means they will be happy all the time. Even when using the more biblical term of joy, there is still confusion about what it means to be a believer who is still living in a fallen world. 'You must know, that there is a great difference between peace, comfort, and joy. A man may have peace that has no comfort; a man may have comfort that has no joy: one is beyond the other, one a degree above the other.

Labor to know the difference between these.' I suspect we spend little energy 'labouring' to know the difference! Instead we tend to run the three terms together so that the absence of one for us means the absence of all three. Bridge further discusses two different peaces, one that 'lies in opposition to what one has been', that is, if we look back on our life before Christ then we would have no desire to return to it and therefore there is a peace in the present despite the struggles we may face. And there is a peace 'that is in opposition to what one would be.' Because we are not yet perfected, we should always have some struggle within. There is peace in knowing Christ as our Savior, but it is a peace that is not perfected until we reach heaven because our own sinful failures should and will bring a lack of peace because we have once again failed the Lord who died for us! Will we have peace, comfort and joy all simultaneously – Yes, in heaven! And we will experience the foretaste of heaven in this life at times by feeling these three together at certain times. But the lack of one or more is not necessarily an indication of a lack of saving faith as some fear, but simply points to the struggle we have with believing not only in a God whom we cannot see or touch, but also in an eternity which is promised in Scripture but otherwise unseen. It reflects our struggle to live beyond our present world of material – touchable, seeable things – to instead live in the presence of the spiritual world around us and in the light of a coming eternity.

Of course, Bridge is not encouraging believers to be content in their condition of lacking peace. So what should the depressed believer be doing when they are unable to find peace in their relationship with God? 'If peace and comfort therefore do not come at once, lay that question aside a little, and in due time, Christ will answer that question too; only now for the present wait on him, and keep his way.' Waiting upon God to respond in the ways we desire is always difficult, but for the depressed person who is already feeling sadness, hurt, and perhaps even some degree of hopelessness, waiting may feel like a cruel instruction. And yet, it is in the act of waiting upon God for relief that we deepen our faith, because we are forced to trust him with his answers in his timing, and we also find ourselves realizing that we do not have the strength in ourselves to live this life, rather we must depend upon God's strength in our weakness. For many, the time of depression is the time when they are forced to realize that it is God's strength and not their own. For those who are not struggling with depression, their faith may appear strong but this can be deceiving as they may be living day by day in their own strength as they are not experiencing the struggles that expose their weakness apart from God. Scripture abounds with historical examples. Moses seeks to free the Israelite slaves in his own power (Exod. 2:11–22) only to fail (Acts 7:23–9). He is left waiting in the wilderness for forty years (Acts 7:30–34, Exod. 2:23–3:22) before God calls and equips him to go back and deliver the people. The Apostle Paul is dramatically brought to a knowledge of Christ as his Savior (Acts 9) but God then sends him off into the desert for 3 years (Gal. 1:11–18) before the beginning of his ministry as the Apostle to the Gentiles. And what of the generations of Israelite believers who patiently awaited the coming of their Messiah, as typified in Simeon (Luke 2:25–32)? Waiting is difficult, but waiting upon God is always rewarded at some point in time (if not in this life, then in heaven) with understanding and blessing.

The other difficulty in waiting is that the depressed person has difficulty 'hearing' God. Much like Jeremiah's words in Lamentations 3:7–8 their prayers seem to go nowhere, to be blocked off and not heard (assuming they are even able to push themselves into praying in the first place!). God often begins by speaking 'a small word' or in quiet ways as Elijah experienced (1 Kings 19:11–12). When Mary came to the empty tomb she was obviously distressed wondering what had happened to Christ's body. Although the angels spoke to her, they were unable to provide her comfort. Finally, Christ appears and speaks to her bringing comfort. 'But what does he say to her? Only one word – Mary. So, when a man is in trouble, the Lord comes sometimes and speaks but a word. Does the Lord therefore speak but one word unto you, yet stir up yourself in believing, and listen to him.'

The task is to respond to whatever word they are able to hear from God, and act upon it. This is comparable to the practical advice often given to more severely depressed people. As their depression deepens, they begin to ignore daily life tasks because they take too much energy to accomplish. But as they then look about them, they see all their responsibilities that they have left undone, and they become more depressed and feel the crushing load of all those responsibilities even more. To help them a counselor may suggest they take one of the incomplete tasks, go home (or wherever the task awaits) and spend half an hour working upon it (any longer and they would fail or not even start because they feel they do not have the energy). This may not complete it, but it does begin to break the downward spiral that they have found themselves in. In essence, the counselor is asking them to 'hear' God speak to them about what one of their daily responsibilities before him would be, and to act upon that, even if they are not currently able to act upon the full list of responsibilities.

SPIRITUAL MATURITY AND DEPRESSION

A common question arises for those that are depressed as well as for those who have never experienced depression – Are the depressed more ungodly than those who are not experiencing depression? Both groups often feel the answer is Yes. But Scripture paints a different picture. It certainly may be that at times depression is the result of sinful actions or desires in our lives. In addition, depression generally opens the door to sinful temptations as well, but as noted earlier, throughout Scripture godly people are often depressed. The Psalms specifically illustrate this as in the heading to Psalm 102, 'A Prayer of an afflicted man. When he is faint and pours out his lament before the Lord.' God, in his wisdom provided many Psalms specifically to help believers when they were feeling overwhelmed and hopeless. 'What a mighty depth of discouragements may the saints and people of God fall into, and yet be godly and gracious.' The evidence of the person's godliness is not whether they ever experience depression but whether they wait upon and trust the Lord in the depression so that the result is growth. Similarly, the Lord Jesus was overwhelmed in the garden of Gethsemane with what he was about to experience – the torture of the crucifixion – resulting in him seeking comfort from his disciples (unsuccessfully as they were asleep!) and praying not once, but three times for this cup (a reference to the judgment for sin he was about to take upon himself for us) to pass away (Luke 22:39–46). Christ was the sinless God-Man, and so there is no sin present and yet there is great struggle. There is no comfort given by others and yet in godliness he does accept and pursue God's will, 'not my will, but yours be done.' While this may not have been depression in the Lord's life, it certainly reflects feelings of being overwhelmed that are common to those struggling with depression. Depressive feelings and discouragement are not, in and of themselves, evidence of a lack of spiritual maturity in the person's life.

While we desire peace and comfort all the time, God's wisdom shows itself differently in our lives. He allows our peace to be disrupted for our own spiritual good. Rather paradoxically, 'for their good they have peace and comfort, and for their good they lack peace and comfort.' When people are able to find comfort or encouragement elsewhere, they typically do not look directly to God. Thus God 'permits a discouragement to pass upon all their comforts; their peace to be interrupted, their hearts disquieted, and their souls discouraged, so that they may encourage themselves in God alone.'

Hebrews 12:6 notes that 'the Lord disciplines those he loves,' and verse 11, 'no discipline seems pleasant at the time, but painful. Later on, however, it produces a harvest of righteousness and peace for those who have been trained by it.' God uses the discouragements, the seeming lack of his presence in our lives to discipline and train us to become more effective servants of God.

DEPRESSIVE FEELINGS

While feelings are important in the believer's life and should not be ignored, they are not always correct in where they lead us, and they do not respond easily to our desire to change them. There is no switch to turn them off or on, nor can we simply will emotions to change, rather we must find God's strength and seek him through our emotional struggles. The depressed person will not be able to simply 'turn off' the feelings of sadness and despair no matter how much they desire to do so. It is at this point that they must seek to deepen faith in order to have faith interact with their feelings. Bridge refers to a commonly heard phrase today, that we do not live by feeling but by faith. He insists we should begin with faith and then have feeling arise from the faith but we typically want to feel before we act in faith. Our example is Christ as he experienced the wrath of God (for our sins) upon the cross and felt the separation that brought, 'Why have you forsaken me?' (Matt. 27:46). But at the same time as he experienced the rejection of God, he also declared 'My God', that is even in a time of rejection Christ still clung to the personal relationship with his Father. We can follow his example, 'though you lack the sense of his love; yet at the same time you may say, The Lord is my Father, and you may go to him as your Father, and if you can say, God is my Father, have you any reason for your discouragements?'

Life is often spent depending upon our faith, our trust in God, through times of darkness when we can not see him. The cross was such an experience for our Lord but he never let go of God even as the darkness of judgment (because of our sin being laid upon him) swirled about him. He is not only our model of how to live through these difficult times, but even more, as the one who has overcome, he offers us his strength as we seek to follow him.

CAUSES OF DISCOURAGEMENT AND DEPRESSION

Moving to the always asked question – where did this depression come from? – Bridge describes nine areas which can become sources of discouragement for believers:

1. because of their sins;
2. arising from their weaknesses;
3. from their failing or non-acceptance of godly duties;
4. from their lack of assurance of the love of God in their lives;
5. from the strength of their temptations to sin;
6. from their 'desertions', that is from those times when God feels absent or withdrawn from their lives;

7. from the afflictions they are suffering;
8. from their struggles with their work;
9. from their spiritual condition not being what they know it should be.

While we may add more to this list today, including depression resulting from biologically based illnesses (but that is partly covered in number 7) or as reactions to medications or drugs, his list remains extremely valid for twenty-first century believers.

Sin

On the one hand, we should be discouraged and saddened by our sins. Not to be so indicates a serious spiritual problem! The sins committed by believers are in one perspective worse than those of the sins of unbelievers, because we have been set free from sin by Christ and no longer are 'slaves to sin' (Rom. 6:15–18). Because of this truth, our sins do bring dishonor to Christ and his work on our behalf. But on the other hand 'if there be a sacrifice for such sin as this, then a man has no reason to be quite discouraged.' And there is always a remedy for our sin because the sacrifice of Christ was once for all for sin (Rom. 8:1, 31–8) and if we now confess our sins 'He is faithful and just to forgive us our sins and to cleanse us from all unrighteousness' (1 John 1:9). This should not lead to a callousness towards our sin or a trivializing of our sin as 'the saints by their sins grieve God, who is their best friend, and therefore certainly they must needs be grieved, they must needs be humbled, or there is no grace.' God is able to bring good out of our sin, including our own spiritual growth, but we should still be grieved that we have violated his holiness when we are now set free from the power of sin. And so we are humbled by our own failure to pursue right living but Bridge insists we should not be discouraged because the object of our sorrow is sin, for which there is an answer in Christ, while 'the object of discouragement is a man's own condition. When a man is discouraged, you will always find that his trouble is all about his own condition.'

His point is that despair tends to focus us inward on our self, on our struggles, our failures, our hopelessness. But confessing sin and humbly looking to God for his grace forces us to look away from our own struggles to Christ who struggled and died but was resurrected to give us salvation and hope. Depression inevitably draws us into our self, focusing upon our struggles and failures and begins to lose sight of loving God and loving others. Being humbled starts with seeing our own sinful failures but then looks outward to God for forgiveness and strengthening and then looks towards how to better serve him in the world, loving others. As an example, 'Cain was discouraged, but Cain was not humbled. Cain was troubled about his condition – "my punishment is more than I can bear" (Gen. 4:13).' In stark contrast, the prodigal son was truly humbled but not discouraged because he knew he could return to his Father and with his confession of his sin, he would receive favor (Luke 15:19–21). Of course, he did not realize how gracious that favor would be as he returned to be a hired servant and was amazed to receive back the status of son!

Weakness

Sometimes the discouragement arises from the person's own weaknesses in their spiritual life.

> I am a poor babe in Christ, if indeed a babe, and so am able to do little or nothing for God. Therefore I am thus discouraged and cast down; have I not just cause and reason for it. No, for 'God is able to make all grace abound to you, so that in all things at all times having all that you need, you will abound in every good work' (2 Cor. 9:8).

Being spiritually weak is problematic as it leaves the person more liable to fall when temptations come (Heb. 12:12), and they find it harder to rise back up when they have fallen. So the desire should not be to stay in a spiritually weak or immature condition, but rather to seek to grow stronger in their Christian life. Moaning and focusing upon their weakness only leads again to the inward focus that blocks out the view of God. Hebrews 12:1–3, in comparing the Christian life to a race, encourages us to run the race by focusing on Christ who has already completed the race. If we focus only on ourselves and our weaknesses we will stop running the race and sit down beside the track where we are. My apologies to those who do run as part of their exercise or physical enjoyments in life, but I have always disliked running (I do like hiking!). It is painful – the lungs gasping for air, the cramps in the side – and so in a longer run it is very tempting to just give up and quit. And most likely I would! But Hebrews urges us at those points of desiring to quit because the pain is too great or the ability to reach the finish line seems hopeless, we should instead focus upon the finish line, upon Christ who has completed the race, and just keep putting one foot in front of the other. Being in last place or being the slowest person on the track is not the problem, quitting because I am focused on being last is the problem. God desires that we finish the race, how fast or how high our placing is never the issue. So the answer for the weak Christian is to keep running, looking to Christ for his strength and righteousness in their life, and not to look at their own failings and thus become discouraged. If they look at themselves the result will be to quit running, which will then bring even more depression as they look around and recognize they are even weaker yet for they are not even attempting to run the race! And then the downward spiral of depression begins – failing to strive forward because of depression which results in more weakness and failure which brings more depression and on it goes.

God knows the weakness in our lives more so than we do. But all believers equally have Christ available to them. Even those of 'weak' faith have an equal share in the righteousness of Christ. Christ's sermon in Matthew 5:3–6 addresses those who are 'poor in spirit, those who mourn.' Christ does not start with 'those that are strong in grace; or those that have full assurance of their everlasting estate and condition: no, but as if his great work and business were to comfort, uphold, and strengthen the weak, these he begins with.' It is not our own strength that produces a strong Christian life but learning to see our weakness and in that weakness to find Christ's strength, 'But God said to me, My grace is sufficient for you, for my power is made perfect in weakness. Therefore I will boast all the more gladly about my weaknesses, so that Christ's power may rest on me (2 Cor. 12:9).'

Victory does not come from our own strength which is obviously lacking for those struggling with depression. Rather, it is completely and fully from God, as reflected in the church of Philadelphia in Revelation chapters 2 and 3. This is the only one of the churches not charged with a specific sin and so are commended, yet they are spoken of as having little strength. It is being strong in the Lord that matters, not our own personal strength.

Deadness in Worship

Discouragement arises when the person has seen how God kept them from falling into great sin and yet when they pray they experience 'much deadness, dullness and awkwardness of heart and spirit.' Their conclusion becomes that God will not accept them because they are distracted in prayer and service. This is a common condition for all of us at times in our Christian lives. We go to church, read the Bible, pray but we feel that it is accomplishing little and find no real joy in these activities. And yet, we recognize that God should be our greatest joy and seeking him should bring pleasure. So we become discouraged at our own inability to experience the joy of being in Christ. Bridge maintains his pastoral approach in responding to this typical scenario. He admits that we should not be in this state and yet rather than be a cause for despair, he once again points to the slow process of seeking God in the midst of our despair. He directs us to three truths to remember. First, that our current state is not the measurement of our future condition. Secondly, 'That you do not cease from duty because of your dullness in it; because duty is a great remedy against it.' Thirdly, that discouragement feeds the spiritual dullness that we are feeling, so fight the discouragement or it will enhance the dullness.

Does reading the Bible seem fruitless and empty – read it anyway. Perhaps read shorter portions and certainly do not try difficult portions such as Leviticus, but seek to read it anyway. Do prayers seem to go to the ceiling and stop, pray anyway, again perhaps in shorter periods of time. Does worship seem empty, keep worshiping and seeking God. As noted earlier, if we stop in the race, if we stop seeking God in prayer, worship, and Bible study then the depression will worsen for now it is true that we are no longer seeking God, we are sitting along the track watching the race. But if we continue, it may be difficult, it may not seem enjoyable but in time God will bring a greater sense of his presence as Bridge demonstrates with his illustration of father and child.

Lack of Assurance

Discouragement can come in a believer's life when they struggle with an assurance of their salvation. They believe they truly asked Christ to be their Savior, but then because of their struggles or the 'dullness' noted above, they begin to question whether they truly know Christ or not. As their fear increases, so their depression increases. There are distinct cases of depressed people who because of their depression and the effects of the downward cycle, begin to fear they do not really know Christ. And because of their depressed state, the assurance they are looking for has to be almost miraculous in nature or they do not believe it to be true. While this is a genuine problem and there is no easy solution for it, the Scripture does recognize that some believers will struggle to grasp full assurance of their faith. But a struggle with assurance is not equivalent to unbelief as some of them fear. 'Assurance of faith comforts, but the reliance of faith saves.' If someone lacks the feeling of assurance, Bridge challenges them to be patient and wait upon the Lord to bring that assurance, while striving to be contented in their current condition. If the person yields to the false premise that I have no assurance of my salvation thus I shall never have it, then he will obviously become discouraged.

Assurance is not necessarily a feeling that is present every day, it comes from a dependence upon faith – believing in that which we can not see to be true! When we seek assurance we usually desire something we can see or touch and sometimes God does respond with a direct action that helps us realize he is present and in control. But more often, he encourages us to believe in the 'darkness' when we cannot see or touch anything. It is then that he points us back to

Christ and the Cross as the ultimate proof of his love and grace. The Cross demonstrates God's character and his purpose and he will not turn away from either. Faith means continuing to believe this today even in the most depressing of situations.

Temptations

Temptations come to every believer in this world. Because our sinful nature is still active within us and we live in a sinful world, the temptation to disobey God's Word is ever present. But temptations should not discourage us, although they may tire us! Bridge addresses what occurs with a person who has been struggling with heavy temptations. They will focus on their many years of struggle with no apparent relief and begin to feel discouraged. But they should not be discouraged because that is the desire that Satan seeks in bringing the temptations. So do not yield to the discouragement 'for then they would gratify Satan and fulfill his purpose.' If we yield to discouragement and despair, we end up fulfilling the very goal that Satan set out to accomplish! Bridge has no desire to lessen the strain felt under the weight of consistent temptations. But he does wish to point to the damaging effect of the discouragement which will eventually become Satan's means to preventing our service and worship at best, and at worst will weaken us enough to make it easier to yield to the temptation to sin.

Furthermore, God is not absent in our temptations. He does allow them to come, but he does not desert us in them (1 Cor. 10:13). God uses temptations to help us overcome the sin that is still within our hearts. Understanding the nature of temptation is vital to avoiding discouragement. 'Tempting times are teaching times' helping us to learn how to live effectively in the 'enemy's country.' Using military imagery, Bridge explains that we are marching through Satan's country and it is now a foreign country for believers. So we would expect times of uncertainty and of fighting. But 'those who are overcome in the skirmish may overcome in the battle.' So a lost battle, a yielding to temptation, is not the final defeat if we utilize it as a teaching time to help us grow in our spiritual life. But if we yield to the discouragement then we become like an army that in the face of defeat throws down all its weapons and 'lies down before his enemy.' Then we will be overcome because we have given up the fight.

Dark Nights

But what of those times when we feel forgotten by God, what Bridge describes as 'desertions.' God is at work in the lives of others around us and they speak forth glowing testimonies but as you look at your own life it seems empty and barren, God does not appear to be present. It appears that 'the Lord has forgotten me, hid his face from me, and therefore I am thus discouraged.' The person feels that they could handle all burdens if only they knew God and Christ had not deserted them, but now it feels as if that worst of all calamities has occurred.

Scripture repeatedly encourages believers by letting them know that Christ will never forsake us and even when he moves away in the sense of us being unable to clearly see and sense his presence, it is only for a time and he will return again (John 13:1, Isa. 54:7–8, 1 Pet. 1:5). Once again the cross stands as a beacon to us of Christ's nature. If he willingly suffered and died for us upon the cross, why would he forsake us now in the present? The answer is that he would not, although it may feel that he has. The true understanding is to recognize that in this sinful world and in our own sinful natures, it is possible to lose the sense of God's presence at times as he is 'drowned' out by the world in which we live. The Medieval mystics wrote about 'the dark night of the soul,' in which we strive forward in the darkness, not knowing where God is at, but knowing we must continue to reach out to and hold onto him in the darkness of life. Depression is certainly one of those 'dark nights' and the answer remains the same – keep reaching out, depending upon the truth we do know that 'never will I leave you, never will I forsake you' (Heb. 13:5).

But why would God ever move away from us for a time or a moment? 'Does he not withdraw himself from them, that he may draw them to himself? Does he not hide his face for a moment, that he may not turn his back upon them for ever?' God's withdrawal is for the purpose of drawing believers closer to him, so that they will truly learn to live by faith in what they cannot see or feel. The feeling of God's withdrawal forces us to seek him all the more. In the time of desertion, believers 'are tender in the point of sin, and they mourn after God. When was man ever forsaken, whose heart was in this frame?'

Afflictions

Afflictions such as illness, poverty, and tragic deaths of loved ones commonly bring discouragement to the hearts of believers. King David reflects this in Psalm 42, as he writes that 'my tears have been my food day and night' (v. 3), so 'my soul is downcast within me' (v. 6), then 'why are you downcast, O my soul? Why so disturbed within me? (v. 11).' Bridge uses the analogy of medicine to explain God's working. A man may take a medicine that causes him to vomit (as in a situation where he has swallowed poison or overdosed on drugs) but we do not refer to that act of vomiting as illness, it is intentionally being caused by the medicine being taken for a good purpose. So too with our afflictions, 'God is always at the back of affliction' using it for his own purposes and our ultimate good. And at the same time he promises to be with us in the affliction so we are not deserted (Dan. 3:16–26, Isa. 43:2).

Isaiah 43:1–7 describes the Ancient Near Eastern trial by ordeal. Someone would be accused of a crime but with insufficient witnesses and evidence to prove guilt or innocence. So the authorities could result to a trial by ordeal. For example, they would find a raging river and cast the accused person into the river. A mile or so downriver they would pull them out. If they were still alive, then the verdict was that the 'gods of the river' were proclaiming their innocence; if they were drowned then they must have been guilty. What a horrible situation this would be to find yourself facing. As an Israelite believer you know there are no 'gods of the river' in the first place for they are just false idols. And you know the danger of the river, how can you survive? God's promise through Isaiah was that 'when you pass through the waters, I will be with you, and when you pass through the rivers, they will not sweep over you. (v. 2).' Does this mean a happy or stoic entrance into the water? No, but it does mean taking with you an understanding that you do not swim alone. The incident from Daniel 3 demonstrates Israelite believers who knew and understood this verse as they were faced with the choice of worshiping the false statue of King Nebuchadnezzar or being thrown into a fiery furnace. They chose the furnace, knowing God would be with them based upon this promise in Isaiah 43. But note they also understood that God's presence does not always mean deliverance in this life, but points to being protected for eternity to live with him, 'if we are thrown into the blazing furnace, the God we serve is able to save us from it, and he will rescue us from your hand, O king. But even if he does not, we want you to know, O king, that we will not serve your gods or worship the image of gold you have set up' (Dan. 3:17,18). God's presence with us does not always mean an end to the affliction, or a miraculous healing from the cancer – it means his comfort with us in the affliction and the fulfilling of his promise that 'He who began a good work in you will carry it on to completion until the day of Christ Jesus' (Phil. 1:6).

Struggles with Work

Believers may become discouraged in their day to day work particularly when it does not utilize the gifts and abilities that God has given to them, or when they find themselves working for a difficult employer.

> Sometimes the discouragements of the saints arise from their employments, work and service. They may be tempted to think that God has done much for me, but I do nothing for God: others are used and employed for God, but as for me, I am cast by as a useless vessel in whom God has no pleasure: and therefore I am discouraged?

But this is never the whole truth for God has called us to much more work than what we typically refer to as vocational work. Service to our family, our church, and our community are equally important. '"There is a three-fold sweat," says Luther; "political

sweat, ecclesiastical sweat, and domestical sweat." A man may sweat
at family work, and it is a great entrustment to be trusted with the
work of a family and this work you are entrusted with.' Work in God's
Kingdom is much more than simply the 'job' we perform each day.
It includes our vocational work but also our marriages, our families,
our churches, our communities – all that we do is the work for the
Kingdom, in which we are called to serve or work for God in all that
we do (Col. 3:24–5). For the depressed person, it may be important
to remind them of this truth, so they do not measure their spiritual
condition by being underemployed relative to their abilities, or
unemployed.

Depressed About Being Depressed

Being depressed leads to feeling depressed! Regardless of the initial
cause of the depression, it becomes difficult to find hope because
the depressive condition itself makes us feel hopeless. But again
the question is one of where our focus lies. 'If a book be held close
to your eye, you will not be able to read a letter of it; but hold it at
a convenient distance, and then you may read it all. So here. As long
as a man is in a condition, and that condition is held close to him, he
does not see his own behavior therein, but at a distance he does. The
Lord removes him to some distance from his former condition and
so he sees and observes what he was and did therein.' Counseling
those who are depressed entails helping them to see the 'bigger
picture' of their lives and of the world around them. Not in such
a way as to trivialize their struggles, but to help them take off the
'blinders' so they can see all that God has done, is doing, and will do
in their lives and in the life of his church. This increased focus does
not automatically remove the depression, but it provides a reality
check because depressive feelings reduce our focus down only to
ourselves and our struggles, thus distorting the reality of what God
sees as he looks at this world. Expanding our focus will help us to
more adequately put our afflictions and struggles into perspective
and be able to fight the increasing discouragement that comes from
being depressed.

FINAL THOUGHTS

How then should we respond to depression in our lives? Is it a matter of simply saying, I need more faith? No, but it is an issue of asking God to deepen our faith in the midst of depression by looking not at the depression or depressing circumstances but by looking at Christ, the 'author and perfecter of our faith' (Heb. 12:2). 'Faith is the help against all discouragements. To hope in God is to expect help from God, to trust in God is to rely or rest upon God for help, and to wait on him is to continue and abide in this expectation or reliance (Isa. 26:3).'

William Cowper, famous poet and hymn writer in the 1770s, struggled with depressive episodes in this life that would last for long periods of time and bring him to the point of attempting suicide. On January 1, 1773, just hours after hearing his friend John Newton preach, Cowper was struck with a fear that madness was going to fall upon him once again. Before his mind became clouded by another bout of deep depression, he picked up his pen to write a hymn of incredible faith in the midst of the storm.

> 'God moves in a mysterious way,
>   His wonders to perform;
> He plants his footsteps in the sea,
>   And rides upon the storm.
>
> Deep in unfathomable mines,
>   Of never-failing skill;
> He treasures up his bright designs,
>   And works his sovereign will.
>
> Ye fearful saints, fresh courage take;
>   The clouds ye so much dread
> Are big with mercy, and shall break
>   In blessing on your head.
>
> Judge not the Lord by feeble sense,
>   But trust him for his grace;
> Behind a frowning providence
>   He hides a smiling face.

His purposes will ripen fast,
    Unfolding every hour;
The bud may have a bitter taste,
    But sweet will be the flower.

Blind unbelief is sure to err,
    And scan his work in vain;
God is his own interpreter,
    And he will make it plain.'[2]

We could wonder if Cowper had read Bridge's book as he so thoroughly summarizes much of Bridge's helpful insights. The very night of writing the poem, Cowper did plunge into deep depression with hallucinations and a suicide attempt. His hymn stands as an illustration of grasping hold of God and the truths he knew about his faith even as the 'darkness' was descending upon him. May we and those we seek to help have the strength to sing Cowper's hymn in our darkest of times.

2 Jonathan Aitken, *John Newton: From Disgrace to Amazing Grace* (Wheaton, IL: Crossway Books, 2007), 217–18.

8

THE DEVIL MADE ME DO IT?

Balanced Reality in Spiritual Warfare[1]

Bring up the subject of spiritual warfare and most likely there will be differing and strong opinions expressed if only two or more believers are present! The main point of agreement is that spiritual warfare is a part of the Christian's life as noted by Paul in Ephesians 6:10–18. The key questions are how is spiritual warfare waged, and secondly as this chapter addresses, do counseling and spiritual warfare relate to one another? Taking the second question first, counseling and spiritual warfare are integrally connected to one another. One legitimate critique of much spiritual warfare practice today is that it is done as some unique spiritual activity separated from the day to day sanctification (and counseling when needed) issues of life. The Puritan writers did not create a distinct ministry activity called spiritual warfare, it was treated as part of the daily

---

1 All quotations in this chapter are from Thomas Brooks, *Precious Remedies Against Satan's Devices*, Banner of Trust edition, 2000 reprint, unless otherwise indicated.

process of spiritual growth for the believer. The first question asked lies somewhat outside the scope of this chapter, but for an excellent treatment of the differing approaches with a biblical solution offered, see *Power Encounters* by David Powlison. In the book, Powlison defends the 'classic' approach based largely on the practice of the Puritans.[2]

Between the extremes of the deliverance approach excesses[3] and the denial of Satan's activity (either outright or by the manner in which life is lived) lies a more balanced approach on how to wage spiritual warfare as part of our spiritual growth process. For this approach we can turn to Thomas Brooks, who like his fellow Puritans clearly understood the activity of our enemy, Satan, as demonstrated in the title he chose for his book and when he notes 'that Satan has a great hand and stroke in most sins.' But he also practically understands that the battle is fought in the realm of our sinful humanity, 'the warfare we really need to wage engages and implicates our humanity, rather than bypassing it for a super-spiritual, demonic realm.' Brooks himself will note that although Satan clearly has his devices that he uses to draw people into sin, nonetheless we must be cautious not to lay blame on him for that which is coming from our own sinful hearts. He goes as far as to state that if God were to chain Satan up so he could not tempt us,

---

2 David Powlison, *Power Encounters* (Grand Rapids: Baker Book House, 1995), 11–13, 25.

3 To briefly recap the controversies in this area, it is helpful to note the differing 'street' approaches of Christians to this problem as presented by Powlison: 'Some people do see a demon behind every bush....Other people I have met grant the devil and his demons such mighty power that their working theology of human evil is "the devil made me – or you, or him, or her – do it."... Some people go so far as to view all the problems of life as demonically animated...Still other people see Satan as a second god, viewing life as an ultimate conflict between good and evil... Today, unfortunately these cases are not oddities. A great deal of fiction, superstition, fantasy, nonsense, nuttiness, and downright heresy flourishes in the church under the guise of "spiritual warfare" in our time... Many practitioners of "spiritual warfare" have good impulses and good intentions. They clearly see the ditch on one side of the road – the follies of the modern age – because they recognize that the Christian life is about spiritual warfare. And they want to help troubled people. But too often they swerve into the ditch on the other side of the road, because the proper curbs are not built into the deliverance-ministry worldview. In rejecting the modern secular worldview they often succumb to the "old pagan" worldview in documentable ways.' Ibid., 13–14.

people would still sin because of their own sinful natures. 'Satan has only a persuading sleight, not an enforcing might. He may tempt us, but without ourselves he cannot acquire us; he may entice us, but without ourselves he cannot hurt us.'

Brooks is well respected among the Puritan writers, 'if readers of Puritan literature were set the task of listing thirty of the "mighties" among Puritan preachers, the name of Thomas Brooks would certainly appear among them, though few would be inclined to include him among "the first three."'[4] Not much is known about his life because of a lack of written biographical sources. He was born in 1608 and graduated from Emmanuel College, Cambridge in 1625. There he would have met with other notable Puritans such as Thomas Hooker, John Milton, and John Cotton. He became a pastor and was preaching after his graduation but we do not know where. By the end of the Civil War, he was the pastor at Thomas Apostles, London (and also was asked to preach at Parliament). He was evicted from his pastorate in 1662 along with other nonconformist ministers. Other specifics are scanty: 'He escaped imprisonment, was eminent among ministers who refused to flee in the Year of Plague (1665), and was at his post to comfort the afflicted during and after the Great Fire of 1666.'[5] During the years from 1652 through 1680 he was writing, with *Precious Remedies* among the first to be written, in 1652. He died in 1680, three years after the death of his wife.

Brooks' approach to the subject is intriguing as he lays out 'Devices' that Satan uses to try to accomplish various differing purposes and then offers biblically based 'Remedies' that the believer should seek to use to deter the effect of those 'Devices.' His usage of the word Devices is derived from the word translated 'wiles' or 'schemes' in Ephesians 6:11 which signifies 'such snares as are laid behind one, such treacheries as come upon one's back unawares. The word signifies an ambush or stratagem of war,

---

4 Editor's 'A Brief Biography' in *Precious Remedies Against Satan's Devices* (Carlisle, PA: Banner of Truth Trust, 1968), 11
5 ibid., 13.

whereby the enemy sets upon a man unawares.' Throughout, he emphasizes the power of the Spirit working in the believer's life and the obedience of the believer to the numerous 'remedies' as the means to effective spiritual warfare with the enemy. While I encourage readers of this chapter to read the entire book, I must admit that Brooks' method of writing makes the Table of Contents a concise summary and almost a condensed version of the entire book!

He begins by challenging his readers to the importance of this subject. 'Christ, the Scripture, your own hearts, and Satan's devices, are the four prime things that should be first and most studied and searched. If any cast off the study of these, they cannot be safe here, nor happy hereafter.' Note the foundation he lays – we must understand what Scripture teaches us and what Christ has done for us. Then we must understand not only the ways in which Satan attempts to thwart believers, but must also understand the motives and desires of our own sinful hearts. Without all four of these areas of understanding, we will fall short and run the danger of the excesses seen in some modern day approaches to spiritual warfare. Continuing, he notes that 'Satan loves to sail with the wind, and to suit men's temptations to their conditions and inclinations. If they be in prosperity, he will tempt them to deny God (Prov. 30:9); if they be in adversity, he will tempt them to distrust God.' Satan studies us before seeking to tempt us, and tailors his efforts to those particular areas of weakness and sin that we may be struggling with. This is why it would be accurate to state that counseling always involves spiritual warfare. By definition, most counseling scenarios involve a person struggling with weakness, sin, and trials which make them more vulnerable to failure. By Brooks' understanding, Satan would be very aware of the specific nature of the struggle and suit his temptations and efforts to those specifics. Recognizing this is a key factor in effective counseling, in order to help the person seek to be alert to seek God's strength in those very areas in which they are struggling, in order to help prevent successful temptation by the demonic world.

'SATAN'S DEVICES TO DRAW THE SOUL TO SIN'

What devices then does Satan utilize to try to draw believers into sin? While Brooks notes twelve, we will consider only a representative sample of them.

> To present the bait and hide the hook, to present the golden cup, and hide the poison, to present the sweet, the pleasure, and the profit that may flow in upon the soul by yielding to sin, and by hiding from the soul the wrath, and misery that will certainly follow the committing of sin.

This is clearly recognizable to every believer, accepting that the intended sin is something good, something pleasant so it can not be wrong. Of course, it is also as old as time, being one of the temptations used in the Garden of Eden by the serpent, pointing to the forbidden fruit as pleasant to eat (Gen. 3:1–6). And I suspect the fruit did look fantastic, and tasted wonderful for those first few bites until the realization of the sin turned it to bitterness. For sin is often pleasant or at least performs some seemingly positive action for us in the beginning. That is why this Device is so effective – it works repeatedly in our lives! But it always ends up in destruction and death just as it did with Adam and Eve.

As will be true throughout, Brooks' Remedies are theological and practical in nature. The first remedy is to stay as far away from sin as we can and not play with the 'bait' that Satan dangles in front of us (Rom. 12:9, Prov. 5:8). 'The best course to prevent falling into the pit is to keep at the greatest distance; he that will be so bold as to attempt to dance upon the brink of the pit' may find that God allows him to fall into it!

How well we know this walking on the edge in our own lives and those of others, trying to enjoy the sin without dropping into it, but of course that effort will fail. If we are not fleeing from sinful situations and thoughts to pursue God we are always vulnerable to that last miss-step into the 'pit.' 'Joseph keeps a distance from sin, and from playing with Satan's golden baits, and stands. David draws near, and plays with the bait, and falls. Remedy – To consider, that sin is but a bitter sweet.' As one who enjoys his chocolates, this rings home because I like my chocolate sweet, and to bite into a beautiful looking piece of chocolate and find it bitter, sets the teeth on edge!

But Brooks instructs us to keep reminding ourselves that this is always the case with sin, it may look delicious and sweet but it will end up bitter in the mouth if we allow ourselves to partake. 'Remedy – Seriously to consider, that sin is of a very deceitful and bewitching nature. Sin is from the greatest deceiver, it is a child of his own begetting (Heb. 3:13).' The greatest con man in history is Satan and so the sins to which he lures us will be quite capable of reeling us in if we do not practice vigilance. As with so many cons today that attempt to promise a 50% or more return on your money if you just do so and so, they look fantastic but you end up losing all your money. Remember that sin is no different, it will promise and even initially seem to deliver but in the end leaves us with nothing but the need to repent of sin once again.

> PAINTING sin with virtue's colors, Satan knows that if he should present sin in its own nature and dress, the soul would rather fly from it than yield to it; and therefore he presents it unto us painted and gilded over.

The Remedy is to look ahead to see how the sin will appear in a few hours after we have yielded to it. Brooks here directs us to the value of both looking forward and backwards. Yes, the battle with temptation is in the present and must be fought there, yet a sense of time is important to effective warfare. Looking forward allows us to try to look at the ultimate consequences of what now seems so inviting. Helping the spouse who is considering adultery to consider the consequences of that action (destroyed relationships, possible divorce, damage to the children from a divorce, having to live on incomes split through divorce, and so on) is not only a needed response of a counselor, but an act of grace. Similarly, most people considering suicide do not attempt to project forward to see how their death will hurt others, they are simply looking for an immediate relief for the overwhelming struggles they are experiencing. But we also have to look to the past, back to the cross of Christ.

Those sins which seem so trivial to us at the time of committing them, are actually immense and costly – they cost the suffering and death of Christ upon the cross. The more we can solidify that critical event in our lives, the more effective we will be at overcoming the 'glittering' nature of sin. In counseling situations, you sometimes find yourself faced with a person who knows they are about to do something morally wrong. But they feel it is the only way they can respond and without saying it verbally, they are thinking that I can ask forgiveness after I take this action! While there is truth in their thinking (rebellious sin is still forgivable) they are betraying a lack of reflection upon the horrible suffering of Christ on the cross for that sin that they are going to ask to be forgiven after they willfully commit it. Reminding them of this fact is not an effort at inducing guilt but rather one to stress the need to trust God when all our answers seems pointless, and to keep on serving him because of his past, present, and future grace in our lives.

EXTENUATING and lessening of the sin. Ah! says Satan, it is but a little pride, a little worldliness, a little uncleanness, a little drunkenness, etc.

What is the big problem? It is just little things, it is not like I am going out to rob or kill someone. Actually, I have too often heard this one in marriage counseling settings (and uttered it to myself as well), 'I know I should do better but it is not like I run around on her or go out drinking or gambling like other husbands do.' Usually, this statement is true and agreed to by the spouse, but it misses the point. It becomes our attempt to trivialize the sin that we are involved in by pointing to other, obviously more severe sin in others. This is exactly the point of Satan's effort. Sure it is sin but it is so small as to not really matter, so just give into it.

'Remedy – First, solemnly consider, that those sins which we are apt to account small, have brought upon men the greatest wrath of God, as the eating of an apple, gathering a few sticks on the Sabbath day, and touching of the ark.' God has not just responded to the 'big' sins throughout history, all sin has consequences and carries a deadly price (Rom. 6:23, Gal. 6:7–9). 'Remedy – Seriously to consider, that the giving way to a lesser sin makes way for the committing of a greater. Sin is of an encroaching nature, it creeps on the soul by degrees, step by step, till it has the soul to the very height of sin.' While not always true that sin progresses in its intensity, it clearly is a general truth. Alcoholics do not start out drinking daily with destruction appearing throughout all of their life, they progress to that point. Most adultery does not start with a sudden jumping into bed with someone who is not your spouse. It usually starts with flirting, secretive meetings, and progresses down the road to further sin. Counseling problems such as anxiety and obsessive-compulsive reactions can be seen in this light as well. The person afraid to leave their home rarely starts at that point but slowly works their way to it over years of becoming increasingly anxious and fearful about different situations until they find themselves trapped. Small sins can and often do follow the pathway into worse, life-dominating sins and struggles.

'Greater sins do sooner startle the soul' rousing us to repentance where smaller sins are easier to brush aside and consider of no real importance. This makes them doubly dangerous because they are allowed to continue in our hearts and work beneath the surface, gaining strength to lead us astray in the future. It becomes key that we resist all sin, rather than yield to any. Church history is replete with the stories of those who were willing to suffer the worst of persecutions rather than engage in the smallest of sins, especially of denials of the faith (*Foxe's Book of Martyrs* chronicles these testimonies). To put it another way, we talk 'big' at times about resistance to sin but fail when faced with trivial sins that do not seem to be worth the fight. Historically, the martyrs understood that even the slightest yielding was failure to honor God and would have severe consequences spiritually.

> Presenting to the soul the best men's sins, and by hiding from the soul their virtues; as by setting before the soul the adultery of David, the pride of Hezekiah, the impatience of Job, the drunkenness of Noah, the blasphemy of Peter, and by hiding from the soul the tears, the sighs, the groans, the humblings, and repentings of these precious souls.

Satan accurately points to the sins of godly people. But he also seeks to obscure the tears and repentance of these same godly men. The Scriptures carefully record both their falling in sin and their repentance from that sin. So the question is raised, 'Ah, soul you can easily sin as the saints, but can you repent with the saints?' I often share with those whom I am counseling that I sometimes use David's prayer of confession in Psalm 51 as my own when dealing with my personal sin. But I have never prayed it as my own without stepping back to observe that David understood the depths of sin and the seriousness of repentance much more so than I do. My sense is that this is what made him a 'man after God's own heart.' It was not keeping from sin, as David certainly was a 'great' sinner, but the way in which he repented is typically much different than our own.

> To present God to the soul as one made up all of mercy. Oh! Says Satan, you need not make such a matter of sin, you need not be so fearful of sin, not so unwilling to sin for God is a God of mercy, a God more prone to pardon his people than to punish his people.

The remedy is obvious – not to deny the mercy of God but to recognize that he is as just as he is merciful. If stated plainly by Satan that we need not fear sin because of the mercy of God, we would tend to draw back and say how terrible, how could any Christian so take advantage of the undeserved mercy of God in their lives? And yet we do. Paul recognized this in his argument in Romans 6:1 when he posed the question, 'Shall we go on sinning so that grace may increase?' and answered with a resounding No, in no way! The answer is obvious but in daily life we often live as if it is unclear. God is a great God of mercy and will forgive our sin based upon the work of Christ upon the cross, but to take advantage of that mercy is a deeper sin than the initial action committed, and displays a desperate need to grasp the nature of God and his work on our behalf. God is both merciful and just. Or in a similar analogy, C.S. Lewis captures this balance in his presentation of Aslan the Lion (his representation of Christ) in the *Chronicles of Narnia*. Susan is asking Mr. Beaver about who this Aslan is and discovers he is not a man, but 'the Lion, the great Lion.' This understanding brings a sense of uneasiness for her which Mrs. Beaver confirms should be the case. This prompts Lucy to reply, '"Then he isn't safe?" said Lucy. "Safe?" said Mr. Beaver; "don't you hear what Mrs. Beaver tells you? Who said anything about safe? Course he isn't safe. But he's good. He's the King, I tell you."'[6]

God is just and abhors sin in all its forms and all its degrees. He is merciful as well, but it is remembering both characteristics of his nature that helps us to battle this device of Satan.

> PERSUADING the soul that the work of repentance is an easy work, and that therefore the soul need not make such a matter of sin. Why! Suppose you do sin, says Satan, it is no such difficult thing to return, and confess, and be sorrowful, and beg pardon, and cry, 'Lord, have mercy upon me!'.

This is just a slight twist on the previous Device looking more at how the mercy of God comes into action in our lives. 'Remedy – That repentance is a mighty work, a difficult work, a work that is above our power (Jer. 13:23)...Besides, repentance is not only a turning from all sin, but also a turning to all good; to a love of all good, to a prizing of

---

6 C. S. Lewis, *The Lion, the Witch, and the Wardrobe* (New York: Macmillan, 1950), 64–5.

all good, and to a following after all good (Ezek. 18:21).' Repentance is not a simple task for the believer, it requires truly looking upon our sinful hearts to see how wicked they are and were in the act of sin, and then seeking to take steps of restitution and change based upon that look. Even with 'small' sins, it is a humbling and difficult task to engage in.

A second remedy is to remember that 'repentance is a continued act.' We do not simply repent at one point in time, rather it should be an ongoing process in our life of seeking to obey God more and more in the future. 'A true penitent must go on from faith to faith, from strength to strength; he must never stand still nor turn back.' This is never more true in the counseling arena than when dealing with 'life-dominating' problems, those struggles that seem to be consistent and ongoing in the person's life. They require the hard work of repentance to be ongoing, not just as a point in time but as a process of life intimately connected with sanctification. Too often the strugglers want to perceive repentance as simply a single point in time, but it is very much an ongoing work in their life, connected to the discipline of putting sin to death daily as noted by John Owen (see Chapter Three).

Finally for this Device, Brooks offers an interesting argument as to the difficulty and the necessity of repentance, 'that to repent of sin is as great a work of grace as not to sin.' When we sin we feel weakened, even fearful of whether God will forgive me yet again. In reality, this indicates that it is a work of grace to repent for we could not do it ourselves. 'Repentance is the vomit of the soul, none so difficult and hard as it is to vomit.' A typically vivid illustration by Brooks, vomiting is a painful and difficult thing to do but sometimes it is exactly what the body needs to rid itself of something which is hurting the body (such as with food poisoning). In this case, the removal (or repentance if you will) is more difficult and painful than the initial taking (the act of sin if you will), which is exactly Brooks' point to us. When sin is identified in the counseling process, the great difficulty of repentance comes next – giving up of the idol of drugs or alcohol or sex or work, giving up the lover who is not your spouse – and usually is very difficult to pursue.

For the truly repentant sinner, however, they do see the mercy of God coming into their lives and interestingly our respect for them also grows, not because they did not sin grievously in their initial actions but because they stayed with the hard process of repentance and rebuilding rather than giving up and yielding to the sin.

> P RESENTING to the soul the outward mercies that vain men enjoy, and the inward miseries that they are freed from, while they have walked in the ways of sin. Says Satan, Do you see, O soul, the many mercies that such and such enjoy, that walk in those very ways that our soul startles to think of?

If you too want to be 'freed from the dark night of adversity, and enjoy the sunshine of prosperity, you must walk in their ways (Jer. 44:16-18).' This one is rarely spoken out loud but I have at times raised the question with someone, 'Are you thinking that living a Christian life has not benefited you in any way so why not pursue this sin you are thinking of?' The honest people at least admit the thought has been present. Actually, what has often been labeled the mid-life crisis may be a variation of this theme – look at the sinners out there who are enjoying life to the fullest (in sinful ways mind you) while I am feeling that half of my life is passed and I am not enjoying anything. The answer seems to be to follow the pattern of the world – trade in your wife, buy a flashy car, take expensive vacations. This is the eighth Device of the enemy.

'Remedy – That there is nothing in the world that does so provoke God to be angry, as men's taking encouragement from God's goodness and mercy to do wickedly (Jer. 44:20–28).' And, again, in one of those unique Brooks' twists that demonstrate his deep understanding of human nature, he writes that there 'is no greater misery in this life, than not to be in misery; no greater affliction, than not to be afflicted.' God's discipline is 'not pleasant at the time but painful' (Heb. 12:11) but will 'produce a harvest of righteousness and peace for those who have been trained by it'

(v. 11b). Further, even though it be difficult to perceive, the wicked are lacking much more than they outwardly are enjoying. This can be seen in the constant striving for more, they never have enough of anything. There is never enough wealth or happiness or health, they keep seeking more. The true mercies come from God and that is what they need to end their search. And so, Brooks reminds us 'that outward things are not as they seem. They have indeed, a glorious outside, but if you view their insides, you will easily find that they fill the heart full of cares, and the heart full of fears.' The old cliché says, 'the other man's grass is always greener' but then explains it almost never is. So too with this device of Satan, the prosperity and enjoyment of the wicked may be true on the surface but it is a fantasy (to them as well as the onlooker) because underneath, everything that they truly seek is missing and there is a great emptiness that can only be filled by living for God.

> PRESENTING to the soul the crosses, losses, reproaches, sorrows, and sufferings that do daily attend those that walk in the ways of holiness. Says Satan, Do not you see that there are none in the world that are so vexed, afflicted, and tossed, as those that walk more circumspectly and holy than their neighbors?

This is the opposite of the previous Device – you Christians are forced to suffer, to forego pleasures, to give away your resources (that others spend on their own enjoyment). It is much too hard a life, why not relieve it just a little by yielding to sin here and there? But we must realize that sufferings are used by God to our ultimate good and we must seek to measure struggles not by how they feel or look at the beginning, but as they appear when at last we can see the final result. The Israelites despaired in their slavery in Egypt but 'when Israel was dismissed out of Egypt, it was with gold and ear-rings (Exod. 11: 2–3), so the Jews were dismissed out of Babylon with gifts, jewels, and all necessary utensils (Ezra 1:7–11).'

Suffering almost always looks dark and empty at the time the person is struggling, but there truly is something on the other side as God completes whatever work he is doing in their lives (Phil. 1:6). Ultimately, the light is in eternity when we are finally in heaven, but God in his mercy also provides blessings in this life as well as illustrated in Brooks' use of Israel's situation. Many counselees bemoan the fact that nothing will ever be good again (and admittedly it looks that way to human eyes) but this sense of total despair is the Device of Satan here pointed out, blocking their view of how God uses trials to bring growth and also how he will bless at a future day those who obediently serve him and keep 'running the race with perseverance' (Heb. 12:1–3). Living by faith and trust today is not about receiving the obvious blessings of God, but about trusting in his ultimate promises (Heb. 11).

> COMPARING themselves and their ways with those that are reported to be worse than themselves. By this device the devil drew the proud Pharisee to bless himself in accursed condition, 'God, I thank you that I am not as other men are, extortioners, unjust, adulterers, or even as this publican'.

The Remedy is to compare our actions (both externally and in our hearts) with the Scriptures which are the true place of judgment rather than comparing ourselves to other sinners. It is not that others are greater sinners that matters, it is that I sin at all. While different sins may have different consequences in life, all sins have the consequence of negatively impacting upon our relationship to God. So all sin by all sinners must be dealt with through confession and repentance. To justify our sin because Adolf Hitler was a greater sinner, makes no sense at all (and in a sense this was the defense tried by various members of the Nazi government during the Nuremberg war trials).

For the final device – 'To choose wicked company, to keep wicked society' – Brooks' remedy is to dwell, till your hearts be affected upon those commands of God that do expressly require us to shun the society of the wicked (Eph. 5:11, Prov. 5:14–16, 1 Cor. 5:9–11, 2 Thess. 3:6, Prov. 1:10–15).' Of course, this is always true. While believers are to be in the world as ambassadors for Christ (2 Cor. 5:20), they must be careful of the relationships they establish. It is a common counseling practice to examine the company that a struggler is keeping – are they people who provide solid biblical advice in their dilemma or people who will encourage them to pursue sinful 'answers' to their problems? 'Hanging' with the wrong crowd will almost always bring the believer down to the level of that group, not bring the group up to a higher understanding and living of truth, as Psalm one seeks to point out in its opening verses. A spouse struggling in their marriage should seek support and direction from others, but too often they seek their advice from immature or even ungodly people who proffer worldly direction, not biblical.

SATAN'S DEVICES TO KEEP SOULS FROM HOLY DUTIES

If Satan can not tempt us into sin, he is equally content to keep us from pursuing our Christian growth, to make us apathetic or sluggish in our service, ministry, and worship for the Lord. To this area, Brooks now turns his attention to describe the Devices used by Satan to produce the result of Christians who are not vital in their spiritual lives.

> PRESENTING the world in such a dress, and in such a garb to the soul, as to ensnare the soul, and to win upon the affection of the soul. He presents the world to them in its beauty, which proves a bewitching sight to a world of men.

Satan will try to convince us that the 'worldly' ways of living are much better than the Christian standard. He may not challenge us to deny our faith, knowing that many of us will not do so. But he will seek to lure us away from vital Christian faith to instead live and look like those whose only standards are the world. So we can end up pursuing pleasure, riches, significance in others instead of in serving God. All of these are commonly met issues in counseling scenarios – seeking to please people, making a spouse, girlfriend or boyfriend an idol, engaging in 'addictive' activities, seeking to please myself first and others only secondarily, arguing that my needs should be met rather than seeking to love others. Obviously, this is an active and unfortunately effective Device some 400 years after Brooks first recorded it! 'Remedy – To dwell upon the impotency and weakness of all these things here below. They are not able to secure you from the least evil, they are not able to procure you the least desirable good.' It is not that believers can not enjoy God's creation because they can and should as a reflection of it being God's. But it is the creation affected by sin, it is the temporal nature of this world's pleasures that Brooks directs us to. Keep in mind that all of this will not last, there is no rental trailer full of possessions behind the hearse as it heads to the cemetery. In enjoying the creation, we must keep the priority of seeing everything in light of eternal things.

PRESENTING to them the danger, the losses, and the sufferings that do attend the performance of such and such religious services. By this device Satan kept close those that believed on Christ from confessing of Christ in John 12:42.

So, first he seeks to lure us away with the pleasures of the world apart from Christ, while at the same time also making sure we are aware of the difficulties of the Christian life. It is such a difficult life, why would you want to pursue it when you can 'eat, drink and be merry?' This perhaps points to one of the dangers in our efforts to evangelize others. In presenting the gospel, too often we describe coming to Christ as the answer to all your problems, the way to perfect peace and joy. While these statements are true from one perspective, they nonetheless ignore the words of Christ that 'in this world you will have trouble, but take heart, I have overcome the world' (John 16:33). And therefore, if not balanced, they make the new believer ripe for this Device of Satan upon encountering struggles in their new Christian life. Rather, we should prepare them for the struggles to come but reassure them that no ultimate harm can befall them in their struggles (1 Pet. 3:13) for God is sovereign over all that we experience. Then too, we have many examples in Scripture of those who, when surrounded by danger, still persisted in serving God and were blessed in their efforts (Ps. 44:19–20, 2 Cor. 6:3–5, Heb. 11:36–40). The Christian life is difficult at times, but in the end it is the only life worth living, 'Godliness is great gain' (1 Tim. 6:6).

> Presenting to the soul the difficulty of performing. Says Satan, it is so hard and difficult a thing to pray as you should, and to wait on God as you should, and to walk with God as you should, and to be lively, warm and active in the communion of saints as you should, that you were better ten thousand times to neglect them, than to meddle with them.

We find the Christian life difficult, so why bother, we may as well give up. Brooks' Remedy is to think about the service we wish to perform unto God, more so than on the difficulty. It is necessary for the glory of God in my life and in front of a watching world, to engage in these disciplines of the Christian life, thus I should strive towards them regardless of any potential impediments along the way. Furthermore, we should meditate upon the incredible struggles the Lord Jesus went through in order to bring us salvation. 'Christ did not plead, This cross is too heavy for me to bear; this wrath is too great for me to lie under: this cup, which has in it all the ingredients of divine displeasure, is too bitter for me to sip off, how much more to drink the very dregs of it?'

Many times we are seeking to help those who are despairing because they have not been able to live as they know they should. It is essential at that point to remind them that it is not in the success of the Christian life that they are measured but in the willingness to keep persevering and seeking today to live as they should. I have often noted that many believers pursue the admirable goal of reading through the Bible in a year. They pick up one of the helpful plans that provide the daily readings and start up in January. For most, by the end of January they are days behind the schedule, trying to catch up, but falling further behind. So they give up on the project. Some may last several months but only a few make it through in a year. My challenge has always been that if reading through the Bible in a year is a worthy goal (and it is!) then reading through the Bible in two years or three years is also a valuable goal! Should we be able to prioritize and focus and keep to the read through in a year schedule? In the vast majority of cases – Yes, so not doing so does reflect some degree of failure. But failure is a poor reason to give up on anything in the Christian life that is inherently worth doing. Pick up the Bible, ignore the dates in the schedule and start where you are. Eventually you will have read through the Bible even if it takes ten years! This is exactly the device that Brooks is referring to – Satan points us to our failures in Christian service and worship and says based on those failures we may as well give up. But giving up is the true failure, starting back up – start praying again, start reading the Word again – is the essence of the Christian life and demonstrates the obedience that will overcome this strategy of Satan designed to keep us ineffective and despairing. Encouraging strugglers to try yet one more time to do the right thing is a key to growth in the counseling realm. After all, it is not really our success anyway, we can only 'overcome' with the assistance of God's power through the Holy Spirit. Our efforts alone will always fall short of true success.

WORKING them to make false inferences from those blessed and glorious things that Christ has done. As that Jesus Christ has done all for us, therefore there is nothing for us to do but to joy and rejoice.

The Remedy is to meditate upon both the passages of Scripture that tell of the finished work of Christ for us and the passages that command us to the duties and services incumbent upon true believers in Christ. When applying Philippians 2:12–13 I find that some overemphasize the first portion of that passage, 'work out your salvation with fear and trembling.' They set out in their own strength to overcome their problems and sins, forgetting that it is only by the power of the Spirit within us and based upon the work of Christ on our behalf that we can 'work out our salvation.' Some, however, overemphasize the second portion of that passage as Brooks here notes, 'for it is God that is at work in you both to do and to will according to his pleasure.' It is only because of God's working in our lives that anything is accomplished towards our salvation and sanctification. Some look at this and fall for Satan's trap, that therefore it does not matter what I do, God will do it all. But by bringing these two actions together – the believer's responsibility with the empowering of God at work – the Apostle Paul is countering both fallacies to encourage us to fully depend upon God while stepping out in faith to obey the commands of Scripture in our lives.

> CASTING in a multitude of vain thoughts, while the soul is in seeking of God, or in waiting on God, and by this device he has cooled some men's spirits in heavenly services, and taken off, at least for a time, many precious souls from religious performances.

Who says that preachers do not know what is going on in the minds of their listeners? Brooks is very aware that as we listen to sermons or as we supposedly join together in the pastor's congregational prayer, that oftentimes we find our thoughts wandering off to what we are going to eat for dinner, or what the impact of the weekends sports results will be, or a host of other trivial matters. These thoughts are obviously distracting us from a focus upon God in prayer or upon God as he speaks through the preaching of his Word. We should seek to remember that we are in the presence of God and his majesty as we engage in worship. 'A man would be afraid of playing with a feather, when he is speaking with a king.' If we do not realize the majesty of the God whom we approach in worship, then we leave room for Satan to 'cast in a multitude of vain thoughts to disturb and distract the soul in this waiting on God.'

In other words, when the thoughts wander, pull them back to the important matters at hand, focusing on and attending to God in the act of worship. If they wander again, then pull them back again. If we do not 'cherish' them but seek to resist them and redirect them upon God, then 'they shall not be put upon our accounts, nor keep mercies and blessing from being enjoyed by us.' Struggle to focus appropriately upon God and his ways and they become just a temptation thrown our way, hold onto them and refuse to do battle with them and they become a successful strategy of Satan as they then become sin in our thought lives.

SATAN'S DEVICES TO KEEP SAINTS IN A SAD CONDITION

Satan can not rob believers of their salvation and their glorification in heaven, so instead he seeks 'to rob them of their comfort and peace, to make their life a burden and hell unto them, to cause them to spend their days in sorrow and mourning, in doubting and questioning.' This truly describes some of those we work with in counseling settings – they seem trapped, burdened down, professing Christ but seemingly unable to find Christ in their day to day fears or despair.

> CAUSING saints to remember their sins more than their Savior, that, as the Psalmist speaks, 'The Lord is not in all their thoughts' (Ps. 10:4).

Instead, we must understand that although we are not yet free from the presence of sin, yet we are free from the condemnation of sin (Rom. 8:1), and from the 'reign and dominion of sin (Rom. 6:14). Consider that the greater your sins are, the more you stand in need of a Savior. The greater your burden is, the more you stand in need of one to help to bear it.'

I often run into believers who see their sin as so great or so repeated (and it may well be) that they feel there is no hope and so they stop reaching out for the grace of God. This is exactly the scenario that Brooks was recognizing in his day as well. His answer is to remember that we are no longer forced to sin, 'slaves to sin,' but we do continue to sin even though we do not have to and should not do so. Thus the ongoing grace of God is desperately needed in every believer's life, as well as an ongoing focus on our Savior, who saved us in the past but is still our Savior in the present and in the future. And no sin is so great that God's grace is not greater. God is even gracious enough to demonstrate this in Scripture through the lives of some of the greatest saints – Abraham failed repeatedly to trust God even as he was the foundation of God's blessing fulfilled in Christ, Moses led Israel from captivity but his sin kept him from the promised land, David was a man after God's own heart and yet he also committed adultery and murder, Peter was the 'rock' but seems to demonstrate failure repeatedly, and Paul spread the gospel to the Gentiles but was himself a murderer before experiencing God's grace of salvation.

For us, the proper balance is to perceive the forgiveness of sin on the one hand, while also keeping watch on the operating of sin in our inner person. Although sin will not be totally removed in this lifetime, it will be forgiven when we confess it. So we can truly look upon all of our sins as 'debts which the Lord Jesus has fully satisfied.' It is key to remember this work that Christ has already performed for us at the Cross, it is relevant every day of our lives. But then finally, the believer will ask, why am I tormented by these sins, what good can come of them? To think about and reflect upon our sins helps to humble us and force us to keep drawing upon the Spirit's help to subdue the sin, being dependent upon Christ to complete the work of sanctification in us. And, although we rarely give it thought, it is 'partly to wean them from things below, and to make them heartsick of their absence from Christ, and to maintain in them compassion towards others that are subject to the same infirmities with them.' Rather amazingly, God can and does use our failures and our sins to help us grow and to make us more effective in loving God and loving others. Good counseling must, of course, work directly with confession and repentance of sin, but Brooks points us to the lessons, the purposes to which God wants to direct us through our sins. Ignoring those lessons leaves the individual far short of the spiritual growth God desires for them.

> WORKING the soul to make false inferences from the cross actions of providence. Says Satan, Do you not see how providence crosses your prayers, and crosses your desires, your tears, your hopes, your endeavors? Surely if his love were towards you, if his soul did delight and take pleasure in you, he would not deal thus with you.

The idea is that if God really cared and loved us, then he would providentially protect us from suffering, evil and even our own sinful consequences. But this misunderstands how God uses things we do not desire to help in the refining process. In addition, it is not inconsistent that the 'hand of God may be against a man, when the love and heart of God is much set upon a man (Jer. 31:18–20).' The subject of providence has been covered in chapter 1, suffice it to say here that once again the conclusions of the sufferer that God must be against me or not able to help me based on what I am experiencing is a common but nonetheless wrong judgment. It is based on our inability to understand Providence.

> SUGGESTING to them that their graces are not true, but counterfeit. Says Satan, All is not gold that glitters, all is not free grace that you count grace. That which you call faith is but a fancy, and that which you call zeal is but a natural heat and passion, and that light you have, it is but common, it is short.

You currently feel passionate but it is just a passing thing, your faith seems real but will soon fade. Here Brooks understands the many doubts that struggling believers experience and which Satan will utilize to try to lead them away to an impotent faith. And Brooks points again to the necessity of doctrinal understanding in order to resist Satan and be able to grow. Doctrine does belong in the counseling setting because doubts not properly met with truth will bring the person down and perhaps end in their straying away from the faith. Properly met, they become a means of resisting the enemy and strengthening faith. Specifically, he points to differences 'between renewing grace and restraining grace.' There is a 'temporary grace' that restrains men from some of their wickedness but their hearts are clearly not changed. When you look at Paul (Acts 9) or Mary Magdalene (Luke 7:36–50) you see a total, life-changing grace. 'True grace enables a Christian, when he is himself, to do spiritual actions with real pleasure and delight. True grace makes a man most careful, and most fearful of his own heart. It makes him most studious about his own heart.' I have often spoken to doubting believers that the fact they may doubt their relationship to God is often the best proof that they have one – the unbeliever is rarely concerned with how God may perceive them, and whether they have failed God or are somehow living as a fake. Those are not their concerns, the presence of the concern points the believer to the existence of a faith relationship which now must be deepened to help answer the doubt that is present.

> SUGGESTING to the soul his often relapses into the same sin which formerly he has pursued with particular sorrow, grief, shame, and tears, and prayed, complained, and resolved against.

He suggests that the frequent relapses into the same sin which was previously repented of, demonstrate the futility of the person's Christian life. Scripture, however, reminds us that the saints often fall back into sins they had repented of (Hosea 14:4). 'Consider that God has nowhere engaged himself by any particular promise, that souls converted and united to Christ shall not fall again and again into the same sin after conversion.' This is one of those common scenarios in counseling, the relapse into the sin. Are relapses a good thing – of course not! But the conclusion that the relapses automatically indicate lack of repentance or even lack of saving faith, is an unwarranted conclusion. It may be that repentance is not present or that the person has never truly trusted in Christ, but that would have to be discovered by further exploration. Relapses are unfortunately part of life for sinner-saints. Does counseling seek to eliminate or at least severely reduce relapses –Yes. But it also recognizes that relapses into the same sin are not uncommon for true believers in Christ.

> To suggest that as sinners we are unworthy, you deserve no mercy whatsoever. Says Satan, you are unworthy of the least crumb of mercy.

Of course, we are unworthy – we did not deserve God's grace in salvation, and we still do not deserve or earn God's mercy in our lives as believers. Too often, strugglers think they are not worthy to be forgiven or for God to give them another chance. I quickly point out that this is true, but it never was and never will be about their worthiness, as all of us are unworthy (Rom. 3:9–31), it is about Christ's worth and his substitutionary death on our behalf. Focusing on whether we are worthy or not opens the door for this Device of Satan to cripple us in our ability to reach out for the grace and strength from God that we need in our present difficulty.

SPECIAL HELPS AGAINST SATAN'S DEVICES

Finally, Brooks completes his book by noting some specific helps available to the believer in the struggle with the demonic world. I would like to highlight just a couple of them which should be fairly obvious but are worth being reminded of in order to help strugglers focus on the important tasks necessary for their spiritual growth and not fall into the trap of focusing simply on those tasks that seem most immediate. He reminds us again 'that Satan must have double leave before he can do anything against us. He must have leave from God, and leave from ourselves before he can cut anything against our happiness (Job 1:11, 12, 2:3–5, Luke 22:31).' Without our permission, Satan can not achieve any lasting success. Brooks notes how in Acts 5:3, Ananias is asked by Peter why Satan has filled his heart to lie to the Holy Spirit. It is not Satan who is being asked why he twisted Ananias' heart. Peter's is asking why Ananias allowed Satan the opportunity to fill his heart with sin, 'as if he had said, Satan could never have done this in you, which will now for ever undo you, unless you had given him leave.'

Further, he brings an historical perspective to the battle by noting that 'God will shortly tread down Satan under the saint's feet. Christ, our champion, has already won the field, and will shortly see our feet upon the necks of our spiritual enemies. Satan is a foiled adversary.' The ultimate war has already been won, but we must press on in the battles that currently remain for us. To that end he offers his specific helps.

The first help is to walk according to the Word of God. 'He that thinks himself too good to be ruled by the Word will be found too bad to be owned by God, and if God does not, or will not own him, Satan will by stratagems overthrow him.' A commitment to and willingness to yield to the teachings of Scripture is essential to overcome Satan. Too many in the counseling room are either ignorant of biblical teachings or tend to ignore all that does not specifically appeal to them. Either of these will leave them alone in their struggle without the very weapon that Christ used repeatedly in his own direct struggle with Satan (Matt. 4). Not to utilize the teachings of the Bible in the counseling setting is to leave the counselee vulnerable to the devices and attacks of the enemy. In an age where the very concept of absolute truth is being cast aside, it is all the more imperative for counselors to bring the truths of God's Word into the lives of those they are helping.

The second help urges us not to 'grieve' the Holy Spirit for it is the Spirit who illuminates to us Satan's efforts to snare us, and provides us the strength and guidance to escape the traps Satan has laid before us.

'The third help: Labor for more heavenly wisdom. Ah, souls! You are much in the dark. There are many knowing souls, but there are but a few wise souls.' We desperately need to teach people how to pursue wisdom. Even when they are open to Scripture they tend to look for formulas and statements that will bring instant cures. Most people tend to the 'black or white' approach where every decision reduces quickly down to one direction or the other. They struggle to discover the wisdom of God which learns how to apply biblical principles uniquely to each individual situation. Counselors are also subject to this dilemma, wisdom learns how to apply the truths of Scripture to the different individuals and situations that they encounter, not simplistically but based on deep insight and discernment.

The fourth help is immensely practical. Resist Satan at the first awareness of his effort to tempt us. 'It is safe to resist, it is dangerous to dispute.' In Genesis 3 Eve debated with the serpent and fell, Job resists and eventually wins out. 'He that will play with Satan's bait, will quickly be taken with Satan's hook (James 4:7).' But circling back to the third help, how can we find the wisdom to recognize the bait and the strength to resist but by laboring 'to be filled with the Spirit.' It is only with the Spirit's aid that we can fight the spiritual war (Eph. 6:12) or we will not be able to stand in that day of battle but will fall. If we attempt to fight Satan in our own resolve or with our own skills and gifts, we will fall before him. 'Satan will be too hard for such a soul, and lead him captive at his pleasure. There is no sword but the two-edged sword of the Spirit, that will be found to be metal of proof when a soul comes to engage against Satan.'

But how do we know when to specifically call upon the Spirit's help unless we 'keep a strong, close and constant watch (1 Thess. 5:6).' Brooks realizes that if we feel totally secure then we are already in Satan's trap. If we do not watch closely for temptations, then we will be unprepared and will fall into the temptations when they occur. 'What need then have we to be always upon our watch-tower, lest we be surprised by this subtle serpent.'

The eighth help urges us to 'keep up your communion with God. Your strength to stand and withstand Satan's fiery darts is from your communion with God.' Is prayer important to counseling? Is a 'devotional life' important for counselor and counselee? Absolutely! It is not my strength that will bring victory in a struggler's life, nor is it their strength found within them – it is finding the strength and wisdom that God brings to the situation.

Precious Remedies is certainly not your typical spiritual warfare book of the twenty-first century but it reflects a deep pastoral understanding of how Satan works to cripple the spiritual lives of believers, and offers biblical truth and practical steps on how to fight against those efforts of Satan. Spiritual warfare writers of today would be wise to first consult this four-hundred-year old Puritan work to develop a more accurate and more importantly, a more effective method of waging warfare against our enemy. Those we seek to help need us to be precise not only about Satan's Devices to lead us astray, but also about God's Remedies to counter those Devices until Satan's final judgment day comes.

CONCLUSION

HELPFUL TRUTH IN PAST PLACES

Every day an article or book promises new insights or new discoveries that will end depression or anxiety or a host of other counseling problems. Generally, these new insights are either totally wrong, represent recycled older ideas, or contain only a small portion of truth. New is not necessarily better when it comes to practical, applicable counseling truth. In the case of the Puritan authors, 300–400 years represents a definite sense of being old to modern readers yet the truths they offer in these books are just as relevant today as they were in their own time periods. Hopefully, that is the conclusion you have reached by this point in reading this book. But before I close the book, it would seem helpful to try to note some of today's counseling problems and which author(s) in this book would offer useful assistance with that problem. Although not all of the applications are obvious and direct, for people struggling with these issues, there is help to be found in the work of the author noted.

ADDICTIVE BEHAVIORS/LIFE DOMINATING BEHAVIORS:

- ~ Owen (ch. 3) describes our battle with sin and the power that sin can assume over us. One feeling those with addictive problems sense is the seeming powerlessness they have. Owen demonstrates how this is both true and false – they are helpless, but in Christ sin can be put to death.

~ Brooks (ch. 7) instructs on how the demonic world will attack those who are struggling and weak but also how practicing spiritual disciplines is the key to overcoming them.

~ Burroughs (ch. 2) reminds us that addictive behaviors are often reflective of a deep inner discontent with life, with others, ultimately with God and the addiction functions simply to cover that inner turmoil. Without contentment, overcoming the addiction becomes much more difficult.

~ Bridge (ch. 6) is relevant because depression often accompanies addictive behaviors because of the cycles of failure and guilt that results from the addict's attempts to solve their problem in their own strength which eventually fails them.

ADULTERY:

~ Owen (ch. 3) provides insight into why people pursue adultery when it is obviously such a damaging sin.

~ Burroughs (ch. 2) is writing about a common theme in adultery, that of lack of contentment – my needs were not being met, my spouse changed, we just were not close anymore.

ANXIETY/FEAR/WORRY:

~ Burroughs (ch. 2) speaks directly to the subject of finding contentment not by having a perfect world but by learning how to depend upon God in that world when it does seem fearful or threatening.

~ Edwards (ch. 5) points us to the understanding that rational thought by itself is not sufficient to bring holistic spiritual growth. Anxious people know too well the irrationality of much of what they feel and do, so Edwards pointing them back to the affections as an area to struggle and grow in is an essential truth. His emphasis on examination as one part of that process is also important as anxious people often do not look deep enough but tend to focus only on their surface feelings.

~ Bunyan (ch. 4) shows others walking through anxious and clearly fearful situations and how they both truly struggle (they can be identified with) but also how they overcome with God's help.

~ Flavel (ch. 1) demonstrates that Providence is always at work no matter how terrible the circumstances may seem around us.

CONFLICT:

~ Bunyan (ch. 4) offers many examples of conflict, with family, friends, other travelers, government authorities in the course of Christian's journey and a glimpse into how Christian dealt with them.

~ Burroughs (ch. 2) can be utilized when conflict reflects an inner core of discontent, not being satisfied with what I have or what others are or are not providing to me.

~ Flavel (ch. 1) provides insights into how providence works to bring good from evil so that even unresolved conflicts can be seen in the overall control and working of God.

~ Brooks (ch. 7) describes how conflict, especially among believers, is a primary tool of the enemy to make us ineffective in witnessing to others of God's power and glory.

~ Owen's (ch. 3) emphasis on sin drives us deeper into understanding that much (probably most) of our conflict involves sin on the part of one or all of the parties involved. Putting to death our own sin first is essential in trying to resolve conflicts with others.

DEPRESSION:

- Bridge (ch. 6) is addressing his entire book to those who are 'downcast' both to help them understand why but also to help them discern how to fight against the levels of depression that truly 'paralyze' people.
- Edwards (ch. 5) presents an holistic understanding of who we are, especially in his denial of the negative versus positive emotions approach. Depression is not always inherently wrong but needs to be worked through to understand its working in our lives.
- Burroughs (ch. 2) offers his understanding of contentment for those whose depression comes because they do not have (or have lost) that which they feel they must have.
- Bunyan (ch. 4) provides examples all throughout Christian's journey of struggles with depression, including how a believer can wrestle with suicidal feelings.

GRIEF/TRAGIC EVENTS:

- Bunyan (ch. 4) again 'leads by example' as he illustrates Christian dealing with the loss of family, then the tragic martyrdom of his Christian friend, and even his own brush with suicidal thoughts.
- Flavel (ch. 1) speaks directly here to sufferers as they attempt to make sense out of the tragedy; without an idea of Providence they will find it difficult to do so.
- Edwards (ch. 5) directs people to the work of the inner person in responding to the tragedies in their lives; not to stoically or rationally try to explain them but to truly seek to desire God and his glory in the midst of tragedy. Tragedy 'pulls' the deepest cries from our soul revealing where our faith is at its weakest, but also opening the door to growth.
- Bridge (ch. 6) discusses grief as one of the causes of despair.

MANIC/STRUGGLES WITH REALITY:

~ Flavel (ch. 1) reorientates us to what is truly reality; we tend to all view reality from our own perspective but it is necessary to seek to see reality from God's perspective.
~ Bunyan (ch. 4) portrays how different characters see reality differently based upon their varying worldviews.
~ Edwards (ch. 5) provides insight through his own process of examination of what was real in the revivals and what was not, and what could not be determined. His process of examination can aid us in guiding others towards how to evaluate their own experiences.

REBELLION:

~ Owen (ch. 3) details the basic source of rebellion whether of adults or children as the power of our indwelling sin that pushes us to our own choices for how to live.
~ Bunyan (ch. 4) provides examples of rebellion in different forms and from different motives but all based on a desire to somehow live independent of God.
~ Brooks (ch. 7) uncovers the motives and actions of the first 'rebeller' – Satan, so that we can better avoid rebellion in our own lives.
~ Flavel (ch. 1) provides insight into one of the most basic sources of rebellion – when we do not understand what is happening and God seems to be silent in response to our questions. Understanding providence helps us in those moments of darkness and silence.

RELATIONSHIP STRUGGLES:

~ Burroughs (ch. 2) leads us toward understanding that no human relationship this side of heaven will fully satisfy us, thus a basic contentment in God is necessary for relationships to be able to exist and function in our lives.

~ Bunyan (ch. 4) demonstrates spiritually effective relationships and their need for true dependence on God.

SPIRITUAL WARFARE:

~ Brooks (ch. 7) is obviously appropriate as this is the point of his entire book.
~ Owen (ch. 3) provides more of the balance seen in Brooks by emphasizing that the basic battle with sin is our ultimate spiritual warfare as the demonic forces gain their strength by the presence of unmortified sin in our lives.
~ Flavel (ch. 1) establishes that it is not a question of an equally good power fighting an equally strong evil power; rather God is all-powerful and the demonic world operates under His sovereignty, thus guaranteeing final victory for believers.

These are just a sample of the common problems that counselors find themselves faced with daily. In each area these Puritan authors have direct contributions to make towards our ministry with people today. While there are a host of 'modern day' problems where direct applications may seem impossible, I suspect a good student would find that indirect application can be found to most of these modern counseling problems because the people involved are truly the same as people of past generations – all struggle with sin in their lives (Owen), all seek a greater purpose for life (Flavel), all want happiness or satisfaction (Burroughs), all have emotional reactions that they do not necessarily know what to do with (Edwards), all are on a journey whether they realize it or not (Bunyan), all experience sadness or the 'blues' at some point in their life (Bridge), and all have a spiritual enemy whether they know it or not (Brooks). So, they truly do speak from the past with biblical wisdom and insight for modern man in all his problems.

May your process of application of these chapters be fruitful, challenging, and helpful to those you serve!